STICKY CONFESSIONS OF A MARGINALLY REPENTANT SHOPLIFTER

A MEMOIR

Tom Bentley

The Write Word Publishing

Watsonville, CA

The Write Word Publishing
Watsonville, CA 95076
www.tombentley.com

Publisher's Note: This is a work of nonfiction. Names, characters, places, and incidents are historically true, though the author's imagination on some chronological specifics might be at question. Locales and public names are accurate to the best of author's knowledge. Any resemblance to actual people, living or dead, or to businesses, companies, events, institutions, or locales is completely intentional. So sue me.

Sticky Fingers/ Tom Bentley. -- 1st ed.
ISBN 979-8-9860928-0-5 (Paperback)

Library of Congress Control Number: 2022910740

To Zack, who was there for the best of times, the worst of times, and the warpings of times.

To achieve harmony in bad taste is the
height of elegance.
Jean Genet, *The Thief's Journal*

Contents

STICKY FINGERS: CONFESSIONS OF A MARGINALLY REPENTANT SHOPLIFTER

A MEMOIR

The hand on my shoulder wasn't wholly unexpected, but nonetheless a shock.

"Son, I think you've got something that doesn't belong to you," came a soft, firm voice.

Heart pounding, I turned, while backing away several feet. Middle-aged guy, suit jacket but no tie, looking expressionlessly at me. I had no thought, just electric fear.

I pitched the bag underhanded at him, hard, and it hit him somewhere around the hip, before he could get his hands up. The heavy 8-track player inside, designed to sit on a table with home stereo equipment, crashed to the sidewalk, shattering something.

I ran. I ran with all I had, despite him shouting, "Stop, wait, hey, stop!"

He might have started running too, but I wasn't going to turn around, and I couldn't hear his footsteps in a busy parking lot off a big suburban street. I was 16, a basketball player—that old guy wasn't going to catch me. But maybe he'd get into a car. Maybe he'd call the cops. Maybe there were cops already at the shopping center.

I ran harder.

It was evening, my clothes were dark. I zig-zagged into the residential neighborhoods close by, pounding down a couple of streets, glancing back, still running, to look. Nothing. Nobody on the tree- and car-lined street, quiet except for the crickets chirping—and the ragged wind of my breathing. I slowed to a jog, then a fast walk, and headed back to my own neighborhood, maybe a mile-and-a-half away.

My heart was starting to slow, and I realized how sweaty I was. My collar was damp, the t-shirt sticking to my back. But I was safe, I was OK.

And I knew I'd steal again.

I knew I'd steal again because the shoplifting thing was working out so well for me. I knew I'd steal again because I'd been seriously shoplifting for my work—yes, I regarded it as a job of sorts—for more than six months now, and the money I was making from selling vinyl LPs, cassette decks and other miscellany to high school friends was turning into small but steady income.

I knew I'd steal again because my circle of friends was impressed with my skills. Some had even inquired about teaching them my techniques. Some were even making special orders.

But more than all that, I knew I'd steal again because I liked it.

This is the story of a many-year period between adolescence and early adulthood where a middle-class Catholic boy—that being me—made it his business to steal objects small and big from stores small and big, with consequences small and big. This is the story of knowing better, of being raised "better than that," of twisting ethical logic so that my thefts were "liberation" and "sticking it to the man."

This is the story of a kid in the 70s who discovered he had a knack for five-finger discounts, so he went about searching for those "discounts" wherever he went. I was an industrious scoundrel, moving from records and small electronics to brief-cases (yes, a teenager with briefcases), clothes and then into liquor. Deeply into liquor.

This book covers my early days of lawlessness, stealing candy from liquor stores as a barely-see-over-the-counter kid all the way to stealing my first semester's worth of books at college. It assays my evolving techniques and props I used in the work, brushes with the law and the courts, my thefts while traveling across country (and across a neighboring country) and finally coming round—after some bursts of conscience—to wondering how I could have been such an idiot.

Oh yeah: my mom finally found out. Forty years later.

Join me on the ride, but just in case, keep your hands on your wallet.

You need to know this: It all started with sugar.

CHAPTER ONE

Sticky Fingers, Literally

Y ou've probably seen a variant of this in some horror film: a trusted character's face, benign and loving, is suddenly revealed from a shocking new angle. Maybe horns sprout, or there's a death's head skeleton seen shimmering within, or a slight smile joins with brimstone eyes into a twisted evil thing. But then the character returns to the irresistible charmer you always knew him to be.

That would be my own happy face as a child, paired with the alternating skin-stripped-away face that reveals, over time, my tormented teeth. Tormented? Affirmative: Present are the teeth of a man who was such a dedicated consumer of sugared objects—the more sugary the better—in his youth that it's miraculous that man still has any grinders left to grimace with.

I grew up in the suburbs of Long Beach, California, a bedrock middle-class kid. My dad worked 40 years at Ford, and my mom managed a couple of restaurants. I was the youngest of two boys and two girls. My parents were, by comparison with others on the block, relaxed in administering their brood.

Ours was a house of noise and laughter, often because my parents let the cadre of my sisters' pals play, shout and eat up the joint. Later, the cadre of my brother's and my pals made the joint jump as well. My parents, amazingly, seemed to mostly enjoy the company. By the time I came around, they were even more relaxed, or tired, or a combo. They probably didn't suspect their youngest had a leaning toward crime, but surprises happen.

I went from kid-hood to punk-hood from the late 50s to the late 60s, and that was a time when the processed foods industry was truly in its ascendance. Convenience foods, like packaged cereals, were, well, convenient. Corn syrup had yet to stab its nutrition-sucking needle in every product under the sun, but there were still many demons in the product aisles. Candy bars were a nickel—five cents for a blast of sugared dynamite!

I blasted, and enjoying the sensation, blasted again and again. My brother and I would eat an entire box (and to you children of now, the boxes were bigger then) of Frosted Flakes at one sitting. Delightful. Across the big boulevard from us, on the humble grounds of a long-gone dairy, there was the Dairy Drive-in store. I would dart across the road with my handful of change to see what Sam, the proprietor, had on offer.

This was when a half-gallon of ice cream cost thirty-five cents. It was not a feat for me to eat an entire half-gallon of ice cream; a dozen doughnuts, no problem. I lived for sugar and its glories. My mother, the beleaguered shopper in this tawdry enterprise, began to despair of both my teeth and her wallet, and she began restricting my intake, but a sugar junkie, even at age 8 or 9, can find a way around obstacles.

Sugar was my soulmate.

Sometimes on special occasions, my parents would relent. I'm getting ahead of myself in the chronology, but on my 13th birthday, my parents gave me a three-gallon tub of chocolate ice cream. They knew I had to face the tremors of teenagerdom cold: armed with my favorite food. Eating ice cream wasn't unlike breathing—it seemed necessary to sustain life. I normally used small mixing bowls; the standard dessert or cereal bowls were simply too small, too trivial, too uncommitted.

I've matured, but my tastes haven't. Ice cream: then, now and forever.

Besides Dairyman Sam, there was a small cluster of shops less than a 10-minute walk from my house, a little strip mall before they were called strip malls. One of the stores sold liquor as its primary product, but it offered a host of other sundries: toilet paper, soap, magazines, and candy. A fine selection of candy.

The store personnel called me the Candy Man, because I would come in and buy 5, 7, 10 candy bars or other treats at a time—again, candy bars were a nickel!—along with a giant RC Cola or two. Where was I getting the money? Collecting soda bottles around my neighborhood and beyond for redemption was one method.

But that was work. Even before the age of 10, I had developed a sense that work was an intrusion on pleasure. Because there was so much residual sugar built up in my system, one couldn't expect me to be rational. It came to me, sometime in second or third grade: why bother with the messy intervention of money when I could just take the candy directly from the store? I didn't fully grasp that the store workers were Candy Man fans, and this was a betrayal. But I had a mission, and wouldn't be deterred; candy they had, and I must have it.

I got the usual "Hey, it's the Candy Man!" greeting when I entered the store. There were usually two workers inside, often both behind the counter, and I knew them all, as they did me. My technique wasn't much, the standard snatch and grab of the untutored. I cased the candy stacks, looked around, and stuffed a few bars in my pockets; I'm sure a Snickers or Reese's Peanut Butter Cups, my favorites, were among them.

Then, heart hammering, looking fixedly ahead, I walked out. Considering I'd bought candy every single time I'd come into the store in that past year or two—and that was many times many—my modus operandi was clearly flawed.

One of the clerks stepped in front of me before I got to the door. "Hey Candy Man, what you got there?" he said, pointing to my pockets. My first public crime, and it had gone poorly. The terrible part was that they called my mother, who came to the store and made me apologize, which I did without really looking up at who I was apologizing too. But the worst was that I didn't get my daily allotment of candy. Fever!

Today I wonder if they'd considered whether I'd stolen before, if they'd discussed my candy habit, once innocent, now stained.

To demonstrate the full Jekyll and Hyde nature of my beastliness, let it be known that I had been and was a parochial school kid at St. Joseph's at the time of my candy store depredations. I was a daily attendee at Mass on schooldays and Sundays too. I later became an altar boy. Thus, having had more than three squares a day of Catechism, I knew what guilt was, and when you were supposed to feel it.

Good thing the Catholics invented the confessional too. I felt the guilt, I confessed it, I felt hungry again for candy. The guilt didn't penetrate beyond my head; when it came to my mouth, I was guilt-free.

One consolation: This time of my criminal masterminding was the early 60s. Snack treats were really coming into the fore. Thus, our house had things like Pop Tarts (nicely sugar coated, though pretending to be healthy) and Instant Breakfasts (chocolate powder, much like Ovaltine, you mixed with milk, but much more sugar than actual chocolate) and Jell-O, which I would make a mix of, tipping the sugar cup with gusto and eating most of all—and sometimes all—of the bowls. I ate them when I let them chill long enough for them to actually become Jell-O; sometimes I just drank the stuff while it was still soupy.

And when times were hard, I'd simply eat sugar out of the bowl by the spoonful. Surreptitiously, of course. Since my parents both worked, there was some period of free time at the house. My sisters paid no attention to anything I was doing, and my brother only intermittently, so I timed my antics.

I also used to just tilt the bottle of cherry cough syrup back and gulp it down, so that it would start a cough, not stop one. Those were the days when over-the-counter cough syrups had codeine in them, so I was getting a double bang for my buck. But at that point, I was always more interested in the "candy is dandy" part of the rhyme.

But there were consequences. Our family's dentist—who conveniently was in the same complex as the drive-in dairy across the street—drove a lovely Jaguar XKE; my regular visits had to have at least paid for its transmission. I once was diagnosed with seven cavities at one appointment. Now, many, many crowns adorn my non-regal enamels. Three root canals. One bridge. Some periodontal work. A hole where an implant should be.

Of course I'm careful NOW. I floss, I pick, I brush religiously. But my candy-crazed mind didn't pay that much attention to my mother and father telling me to do those very things back then. Today, I still love sugar; I just don't eat it in the quantities I did. I'm much choosier now, going for the good chocolate, the high-end confections. I don't eat dessert after breakfast and lunch anymore (though after dinner is still necessary).

But sometimes, when I eat a small bowl of good ice cream, I can still feel the fever of my old self heating up—I KNOW I could eat a half-gallon again, delirious, inward-eyed, my soul glazed and syrupy.

I don't want to be one of those hovering protectors, preventing kids from having a nice dessert, an ice cream on a summer's day, but for some kids like me, man, that stuff should have come with a warning label.

Because by the time my teenage years were opening up the throttle, candy was merely the top of the snow cone, a warm-up of lootings to come. My thieving hands should have come with a warning label.

Keep that confessional warm, Father.

CHAPTER TWO

It's a Dirty Job ...

I was somewhat chastened by my embarrassing record of criminality from the liquor store experience, and probably more chastened that my mom had to stage the guilt intervention. I don't think I went into that store for close to a couple of years, so I even lost my Candy Man designation, though not my appetite.

Lucky for me there was Ryan's Drugstore up the street about the same distance as the liquor store, but in the opposite direction, so my needs could be fulfilled just as quickly. By the time I was 11 or 12, I was getting a weekly allowance, possibly a dollar. I never learned to save, a debility that marks my life to this day, but I didn't spend it all at once on my candy fevers; I'd space it out over a few days.

I don't ever remember stealing from Ryan's in that period, though I have a strong memory of Mr. Ryan giving me a sweepingly disapproving look when I came in with a dress on and eye makeup for a Halloween party when I was 11 or so. I thought I was a lovely flower of womanhood, but when I brought my cache of Jujubes, M&Ms and Good and Plenty to the counter, he mumbled something like "That's not right," to me, and callow naif that I was, I didn't quite get what he was alluding to, though I understood it was bad, and I was the source of the badness.

So, I could buy some candy, but because I had to buy other necessities like comic books and X-Ray Specs from the back of comic books, I still felt the pinch of penury. All that good Catholic education—I was still at St. Joseph's—couldn't quite whisk the allure of sin from my festering mind. I periodically began to take a small amount of change—a quarter here, forty cents there—from my mom's purse or from where my father put his change and wallet when he came back from work, reliably above the kitchen counter in a cupboard, to keep the candy supply steady.

That I turned out to be the bad seed in the family is interesting, particularly in that both of my parents were upright without being uptight. They were both honest, never running afoul of the law, genial and open with their friends, reasonable—though as kids, we wouldn't always agree—with me and my siblings. I didn't have a model of an appealing sinner to adulate and imitate, unless you consider Satan, but he was out of my league.

But my interests in being not-quite-honest didn't wane.

I learned how to skulk around silently, even when my siblings and parents were in our small house, sometimes nabbing some change when they were in the opposite room. There was a frisson of thrill there, but always a buzz of guilt, too.

But not enough to make me stop.

Oh no, there was no stopping. There was only escalation.

There had to be a safer way to ensure my daily sugar allotment was met. You might remember those dark-blue, square, folding coin-collecting books that had slots for the coins. My parents had given those to my siblings and me years back, and they'd let us go through their coins when they came home from work. We worked on those collections for years, books of pennies, nickels, dimes, quarters and even half-dollars. We had nothing actually rare, but there were some nice old coins in those collections.

"Were" is the word: after a time, my father stored the semi-full books in our attic, and when I had a chance, I began taking them down and filching the coins to feed my sugar flame. Before it was discovered that Little Tommy was on the take, those books went down to about 1/2 of their original weight. Candy! Candy called to me, the sweet siren song, coin collections be damned. Clearly, larceny played a part in my pleasures, and that became a developing interest, further confirmed with each instance.

But not without some shame. The family (my parents and three siblings, all older and less maniacal about sweets than me) didn't take kindly to the information that I was using coins from a mildly amusing family pastime to pay for unwholesome amounts of candy. From those years of Catholic school, I was still damp from soaking in tubs of guilt, and I got the stink eye from all for my coin-snatching antics. So the much-lightened coin collection went back in the attic. And I had to ponder in my own attic of my mind where my next fix would come from.

Gradually, my allowance went up, but not enough to fulfill my deepest sugar interests. So I had to develop a parallel interest: stealing liquor from my parents, and from the parents of friends. By age 13, I'd made friends with some kids that lived down the street. One, Zack, was a bit younger than me, but seemed exotic, in that rather than the working-class parents I had, his were college educated. Zack's dad was a psychology professor at the nearby university and his mom also worked in that field. That his parents kept a close eye on Zack's doings at home made my looser home atmosphere appealing to him. He could come over to my house and watch the gory shows—"Combat," "Rat Patrol"—that his folks felt weren't culturally enriching.

Or he could go over to Matt's, our other friend's house. Not only did Matt's house have the television on all day, they had three or four televisions on all day. Matt's father was a lawyer, and the expansive grounds of the house, the pool, and the nicer cars all said that Matt's dad had the bucks. He also had the liquor cabinet.

Now my parents had a liquor cabinet too. But it was stocked with half-gallons of the cheapest booze. Popov vodka, Early Times whiskey, some gin if not born in a bathtub then born of a bathtub's second cousin. Brew 102 beer, when the company should have quit at 101.

However, the advantage of my parents' liquor cabinet was volume: you could steal (and by this, I mean I could steal) a half-pint of liquor out of a half-gallon bottle without it being too noticeable. Particularly if you put some water back in the bottle. This was terrible booze anyway, so we were doing my parents a favor. Kind of.

Matt's father's liquor cabinet was much more interesting. Matt's father liked a drink, and he liked to entertain as well. So he had premium liquors, and many mixers and liqueurs. When Matt's parents weren't home, we'd pull out the little bottles of liqueurs and try them. Since many of them were sweet, that only fed my fancy.

We found a dusty bottle of Pinch, at that time a high-end blended Scotch, back in his cabinet, and had a fine old time pretending we were sophisticates. He also had a bottle of Old Weller 107, opened, thank God, so we could have little sips of a big bourbon. That bottle now would go in the four figures.

Both of those spirits would affect some of my later beginner's drinking—and corresponding shoplifting. This bit of playacting was also a rehearsal for the cigar-and-wine phase Zack and I enacted later.

Not only did Matt's dad have an exotic liquor cabinet, he and his mom had a bounteous freezer. Whereas we might have a single half-gallon of cheapo ice cream (or sometimes two, because I ate the stuff so quickly there had to be a backup) in our home, Matt's family—which included an older brother and sister—would have five or six different kinds of ice cream. And not just ungainly half-gallons: they had pints of premium ice cream, like Baskin-Robbins, and multiple flavors. This was before Haagen-Dazs was shipping its pints around the country—having Baskin-Robbins in the freezer meant you'd made it. At least to a sugar-fiend kid.

So, stealing from my parents was guilt-inducing. But stealing from my friends' parents? Now that I had confederates in crime, I felt a bit more comfortable, more justified, less sober. We reinforced each other's behavior. If my parents were home, we could go over to Matt's and see if they'd stepped out. Zack's parents would step out too, but they were more discerning about what went in and out of the pantry. They weren't buying vodka by the half-gallon either.

We were classic latchkey kids at the time. My parents both worked, as did some of my friends' parents, so we'd get home from school mid-afternoon to an empty house, grab a bite, and see what the others were doing. Most of the time it was pretty innocent, playing baseball or hide-and-seek with all the other neighborhood boys and girls—my brother, Zack, Matt, Janet, Judy, Micki, Ricky, Rich—who were all fairly close in age, riding our bikes around, having dirt-clod fights, yelling back at the neighborhood drunk, Diane, who came out in her yard to yell at us. We spent hours together, only reluctantly going home for dinner after hearing parents call up and down the street. Seemed all good to me.

Though some antics had the potential to be not so good. Next to the Candy Man store was a laundromat, and because kids will wander anywhere they have no business, we used to wander in and out of that establishment when we'd finished our depredations at the liquor store. One Saturday morning my brother Rick, Zack and I went in, and I had the sizzling inspiration that I should crawl into a big dryer, and they would shut the door and start it up.

This surely proves that candy is as good for your intellect as for your teeth. Dryers, not designed for a mid-sized 13-year-old boy, nonetheless could accommodate one. I did strugglingly crawl in, they did shut the door—which latched from the outside, without compromise—and started it up.

And then they left.

They didn't set it on the highest temperature, but it was set to dry, and it did indeed begin to rapidly heat me up, while tumbling me around. This was amusing for perhaps 30 seconds, until I realized that I would soon reach the temperature where my brain's popcorn kernels would start popping. Now I was scared.

I tried to push open the door, while yelling, but that only brought more tumbling and hair-crisping. I was more scared, and starting to panic.

I was close to using both my legs to crash the latch from inside when the door popped open. Who saved me? None other than the proprietor of the establishment, who was as hot as I was that a big kid was in his dryer. He pulled me out by one of my legs and dressed me down with some loud language, and I quickly scooted out of the shop. Hey, why was he so pissed? Rick and Zack had paid for the dryer time.

Sometimes being daring was fun, but sometimes being daring was actually being stupid. On my 12th or 13th birthday, out of the blue, my father presented me with a heavy, bolt-action .22 rifle. It was an old weapon even then, a gun with a weighty, nicely grained walnut stock and long barrel. It had a tube-magazine that slid out of the rear of the gun, which if I remember rightly, held 10 rounds. My father probably gave me a short lecture on gun safety that undoubtedly never even entered my ears as I warmheartedly hefted the old weapon.

I loved it. I loved the fact that I had a gun, and that none of the other kids in the neighborhood did. And that's what I was—a kid with a gun. And you thought the suburbs were safe. But I was dedicated: I immediately bought a cleaning kit that had long barrel bristles that I'd soak with the cleaning oil, and ram up and down that barrel until there was some small reduction in the dark grit that always seem to endure despite every cleaning. I bought a nice zip-up case. I practiced clapping open and shut that single-shot bolt over and over in my room, aiming it at objects in my imagination.

On more than one occasion, when no one was around in my suburban home, I took the gun out in the backyard and shot it into the dirt near our fence, and once up at the top of the telephone pole behind our house. Our house was behind fairly high fences, and I never heard a neighbor's cry of "What's going on back there?" They probably thought it was just firecrackers or a cap gun, a boy and his toys.

That was madness enough, but once I chased my brother down our street with it when my parents weren't home, with some of my friends around. It became a legend of sorts, but I don't remember that it really *was* loaded.

[Note to the brother I have yet to shoot: I'm sure I had the safety on, Rick.]

Suburban warfare aside, I was still interested in candy. Though Zack wasn't the sugar demon I was, he still appreciated the stuff. We had an early co-dependency. We'd go to my Candy Man store (having avoided the store for years, with time and employee changes, I was on good grounds with them again), load up, and then go back to my room, close the door, and eat everything we'd brought back in our laden bags. That would mean several candy bars apiece, Big Hunks and Paydays, and maybe packages of random candies like SweeTarts or Hot Tamales, or M&Ms and Fizzies, all washed down by a 16-ounce RC Cola. I called these occasions "Celebrations."

One aside about RC Colas. I took an odd pleasure in fancy glassware, going back to age 10 or so. Perhaps it originated in seeing James Bond villains sneer while they swirled their brandy. My parents (and my siblings) probably rolled their eyes, but for a while I drank all my soft drinks out of a giant brandy snifter, where a fizzing 16 ounces of soda was only twenty percent of the glass's capacity. I thought it was dashing.

I was pretty indiscriminate about the candy: give me Necco wafers, Kit Kat bars, Mallo cups, bubble gum cigarettes, Bit-o-Honey, Abba-Zaba, hard candies, soft candies, even non-candies, like Sen Sen.

(Well, I take that back about Sen Sen. I did try a pack now and then, dimly not realizing that their strange, soapy taste wasn't really a candy, but a breath freshener. I'd rather my breath smell like gym socks than Sen Sen.)

The Celebrations were benders, essentially. Of course, I was so sugared-up that I hardly wanted to eat anything at dinner. Vegetables? Get thee behind me, Satan!

CHAPTER THREE

Literary Tastes That Weren't So Tasteful

At age 14, I was still in Catholic school, though I'd graduated from grammar school to high school. St. Anthony's was a bus ride away, almost to the heart of Long Beach's downtown. I was no more pious than your average 14-year-old, which means not pious at all. This was 1968, a tumultuous year, one of Martin Luther King's assassination, then Bobby Kennedy's. There was the mad, vile 1968 Democratic convention. There was Nixon and the ongoing Vietnam war.

I had a budding political consciousness, based mostly on budding-hippie outrage, but that grit in the oyster merely simmered: mostly I was just 14, living in the suburbs, and going to Catholic high school. My two sisters and my brother all went to St. Anthony's as well, but my sister Kathleen bailed after her first year for public school, as did my older brother. However, my sister Colleen was a lifer, and made it through without Satan tempting her to those wicked public schools.

Though you didn't have to be going to public school to be wicked. One of the first things I learned at St. Anthony's, besides a little Latin, was that the vending machines in the courtyard could be inveigled to give up their goods. Though, if

I remember right, it was just one vending machine, but for a kid with an eye (mouth, really) for candy, that was enough.

This machine had those cylindrical chromed-metal pull-handles that brought the candy to you in the tray below after you deposited your coins and pulled the handle. This one was much more generous: don't bother to deposit the coins, but pull the handle very hard, and the candy would roll into your welcoming hands.

The deal with this machine was that it was just one of the five or six handles that did this, and the candies that were always in this particular slot were things like LifeSavers, Wint-O-Green mints, and other similar hard candies. So, not anything precious like a Mars bar, but still free. I can't remember who discovered this phenomenon (I like to think it was me), but I took advantage of it: I would get three or four rolls of candy for myself, and sell others at a discount to other students. Of course, I sometimes gave away freebies too, to become known as a benevolent merchant.

Oh, added value: If you vigorously crunch Wint-O-Green mints in a dark place, anyone venturing to look into your mouth will see them spark. This is not an urban legend, but a phenomenon called *triboluminescence,* where electrons get a little jumpy. Many hard candies will do it, but oil of wintergreen is actually florescent, so the mouthy flash is magnified. Ahh, science.

I didn't sell the candy that often, but I did do it enough to get my first small lesson in business ethics: namely, that there are no ethics when you are in business. It would take some time before the darker aspects of that thought were truly put into practice, but that was much further down the line. At some point, whatever custodian or candy-delivery employee filled that machine figured out that its mechanical soul was corrupt, and they fixed it. But not before I'd had a very good run.

One other thing that St. Anthony's had was sexual segregation: we lads were at St. Anthony's for boys, and the parallel universe of St. Anthony's for girls was across the fenced-off courtyard, though visible to us boys. This of course made their domain more interesting. At St. Joseph's, my grammar school, the classes were mixed: boys and girls. Some of the nuns or lay teachers separated us on opposite sides of the classroom, but mostly we were mixed together, so that the fascination of a mole on the neck of a girl sitting in front of you might keep you from hearing a single word of the math lesson.

At St. Anthony's I could only imagine the lissome necks of my female fellows and look longingly at them from a distance (and imagine they were returning the longing looks). Why were thoughts of girls tangling with thoughts of sugar? As with the Wint-O-Green spark revealed above, science. The science of hormones. I had become the ickiest of things: a 14-year-old boy. Not something you want around the house or yard.

Because I was lacking in fundamental social graces, I hadn't had a girlfriend yet. Or a first kiss. Unless you count a distressing game of Spin the Bottle our neighbor kids had when I was 11, and one of my friend's older brothers, perhaps 13 at the time, gave me a long, sucking kiss on the lips, and I fell away breathless and astonished. I didn't know what kissing was about, but I didn't think I wanted him kissing me.

Back to girls: they remained marvels to me, but marvels at a distance. How would I ever get close to one? Of course, there were a few neighborhood girls that we played with, and even, after studied positioning, bumped up against in Matt's pool, but I was thinking back then of a real prospect. Could I learn manners, discern subtle cues from speech, read body language and finally connect with a girl?

No.

But I could steal pornographic novels. So I did that instead.

At that point, I hadn't been stealing anything for a while. As I said, I was back in the good graces at the liquor store down the street, though they didn't call me the Candy Man anymore. Even though I still bought a great deal of candy from them: not a pound at a time as I had when I was 10—at 14, perhaps a mere half a pound. I was a known but fundamentally anonymous customer.

Being the literary type, I had scanned the racks of paperbacks they conveniently had set in short rows near the store entrance. Aside from the pulp novels, westerns and commercial blockbusters, they had porn. After spotting one in the rack, I began to recognize the cover style of the publisher: a nearly blank cover, sometimes with a wispy illustration, but mostly just a title: something like "Getting Over the Hump," or "Two Stiff Ones and a Lube."

I'm not kidding. You would have to make an effort to come up with lamer titles, but no one at the publisher was making any effort. The publisher's name was on the back, and it was probably something like "Fantasy Lane." But I didn't care what was on the front or back covers. There was actual naughty stuff inside, even if a lot of the language was laughable, with many a "throbbing shaft" and a "wet gash" and other poetic tropes. But there was a great deal of fucking, on beds, against walls, in elevators, on staircases. As well as a great deal of shuddering orgasms, with great sprays of dampness from all parties.

I found it all tasteful and delightful. So much so, I began stealing the books from the store over a period of weeks or perhaps months. The first time I did it, after glancing around the racks at the store counter, I stuffed the book down the front of my pants and pulled my t-shirt back over. Considering I was stealing a porn novel, the pants bulge was a nice touch that I only thought of later. Later I refined my technique by slipping the books under my arm while wearing a jacket. This technique, with refinement, would come in handy—very, very handy—when I later kicked my shoplifting into a higher gear.

I read these works of literature more than once, but certainly not more than four or five times. I kept them high in my closet, behind and under things like puzzle boxes or folded sweaters or old toys. Considering I shared a room with my older brother, that wasn't as easy as you might think, but concealing things in that area of the closet became one of my mainstays later on. My parents trusted us, and didn't go through our things.

As I'll explain in some detail later, that latitude, which I didn't earn, brought me to the edge of calamity many times. Mom, you gave me a good upbringing and never showed me an example of how to stray from the good path. I had to seek the dark path on my own.

I'd keep a novel for a week or two and then give it to one of my pals. Probably Matt, to pay him back for letting us look at his father's Playboys, another luxury of his household. After a while, I tired of all those manhoods and all that throbbing, and I went looking for other diversions. They were out there. As I mentioned, my buddies Matt and Zack lived down the street from us, on another suburban street that was perpendicular to ours. Where their street met mine, Zack's was to the right and Matt's to the left.

It was a typical suburban neighborhood of the mid-60s in Southern California. Mostly white, mostly families with a couple or more kids, middle of middle-class. Quite normal in the daytime. But a couple of times, Matt and Zack and I made it quite abnormal after the midnight hour. I'm uncertain whose idea it was, but we snuck out, took a gallon can of gas and poured it from one edge of my street toward the end of the road where it met Matt's and Zack's street. And then we lit it.

This was quite satisfying: this put up a fence of fire in the middle of the street, which shimmeringly held for a number of seconds before it flamed out. For us, standing perhaps ten feet back on the sidewalk, it seemed to illumine the street like it was daytime. I'm yet astonished that no one in the neighborhood happened to either wake up from the unearthly flare, or was up and saw their curtains aglow. This was a completely unsafe thing to do (part of our motivation, of course), particularly because people had their cars parked curbside.

Now that I think about it, it was probably Matt whose idea it was, since at that time in his life he had never seen a fire he didn't like. He made small bombs out of cut-off match heads stuffed into metal film canisters. He experimented with inventions like this in the pool room, which was part of their garage they'd converted to house a pool table. He did manage to light part of the floor on fire once.

We were all pleased with fire. A year or so after the street flamings, my brother, Denny, Zack, and perhaps Marty and Matt too spent an evening a short time after Christmas in my parents' station wagon picking up multiple loads of dried Christmas trees that homeowners had put out as trash. We piled up a large pyre of them in the parking lot across the big boulevard that flanked our street, poured some gas over them, put down a gasoline fuse, lit it and ran. The dried trees ignited in a big "thump" with enough ignition pulse to feel the heat blow on our backs as we ran.

From across the street, hiding in the bushes, we could see the flames go up at least fifty feet, with several fire trucks coming to douse it, though it died down quickly. Parents, remember that when Sally Sue says she's going over to Doris's to do homework, they might be playing with matches.

And another "idiot gods of fire" story: we used to have big dirt clod fights where many of the kids of the neighborhood ran around and threw clods at each other, picked from the various house yards.

I'm unsure whose idea this one was, but it might have been mine: At least Zack and I—maybe Matt too—were in my backyard, and someone came up with the idea of soaking clods in gas, lighting them, and throwing them toward another one of us. Everyone was wearing work gloves, so we could catch them and crush them into tiny fires. Then one of us had the idea of throwing some on the roof of the house next door, which was vacant at the time. I won't claim this idea, which was titanically stupid, but I did participate.

We threw a number of clods, that burst into tiny clusters of flaming clods, on that roof. Remarkably, it did not catch fire. We stopped after a bit, perhaps because the bright idea that this was highly inadvisable came to one of us. Teenage boys: there should be legislation against the concept.

Because we're heated up now, I have to tell one more fire tale, because even though it breaks the chronology, it has a shoplifting component too: a couple of years later from these adolescent pranks, I was hitchhiking back from Seattle alone and was picked up by a woman and her very young daughter in Ashland, Oregon. While she was on the outskirts of Ashland, she also picked up another hitchhiker, a giant guy who upon hearing that the woman had little money and was fleeing a bad relationship, offered to supply all food for the ride: "I'm a great shoplifter, no problem, I can get anything."

Well, humph! I looked him over, and decided that because he was about 6'4" and 335 pounds, he probably could have stowed away a turkey or two in his clothes. But I questioned his style and skills immediately. I didn't have time to see him in shoplifting action, because not long after we started to ascend the mountain roads leading out of Ashland, the car stalled. The ride was a 60s Ford, either a Falcon or a Comet that seemed in OK shape, but the engine didn't take to Ashland cresting.

The big fellow, after declaring that he was a mechanic also, siphoned a bunch of gas from the tank into what looked like a quart mayonnaise jar from the trunk. He told the woman to crank the engine while he poured the gas in the carburetor, which he'd exposed by taking off the air filter. She turned the engine over a couple of times and then all hell broke loose.

A backfire caused the gas to ignite, lighting the surface of the engine on fire, and our mechanical genius threw the lit jar—which broke—onto Highway 5, into three lanes of moving traffic. The gas threw up a two-foot line of flame, and though it only lasted a few seconds, several cars drove through, the drivers' faces petrified with fear. I guess they didn't want to stop and take their chances with us. The engine fire quickly went out too.

I then said, with what I thought was sympathy and practicality, "Well, I don't think this car's going anywhere soon." I figured I'd just hit the road: I had no money to help, no mechanical skills, and I thought they were all crazed, so I figured to exit gracefully. Wrong.

The car's owner looked up at me with Lucifer in her eyes. "What!" she screamed. "This is a great car! I paid $150 dollars for this car, and it's going to get us to LA, you bastard!" I said nothing while I got my stuff out of the car, and moved down the highway, so that I could start hitchhiking away from them. The flaming gas on huge Highway 5 did remind me of our early days on my home street, though we didn't have that kind of traffic. And it taught me not to trust what shoplifters say either.

And there is playing with fire of a different kind. Back to when Zack lived down the block: Right at the junction of my, Zack's and Matt's streets was Diane's house. Diane was a scary drunk who lived alone, except when one of her odd boyfriends might scuttle in or out.

She was probably only in her forties, but going on seventies to us, skinny, blotchy complexion, raggedly long, dark witchy hair. We often played baseball, using the manhole cover that was on the street in front of her house as home plate. We laughed, yelled and screamed, and while that was tolerated by most of the parents in the neighborhood, Diane often took exception. She'd come out on her front porch and rail at us, "You kids shut up and go home!" and worse. Other times she'd come out and be syrupy sweet, offering us ancient, bad candy and praising us for things she knew nothing about. We figured the variation was whatever temper of demon rum she'd had that day, or if she was on her way up or down.

One time when we were playing hide-and-seek, with the light pole near her house as the tagging spot, I ran into Judy, our pal Janet's sister at full speed as we were both veering to the pole to be the first to touch it. We violently cracked heads, and I went down and perhaps even lost consciousness for a moment. I awoke to have Diane's tangled locks dangling down into my face, and worse, her booze-fouled breath asking me if I was all right. Diane's face was not a cure for a headache.

One of my early-boyhood friends from right across the street from my house was Denny, who occasionally played baseball with us, but often just hung out, sometimes playing his guitar and singing. He had a decent voice, and he knew some old songs from the 40s and 50s from his dad's records, Sinatra and Dean Martin and singers of that era. One early evening he was out there playing his guitar and singing while a bunch of us were hanging out and Diane invited him back into her house. Even though Denny was a bold guy, he wanted company to go into Diane's dark cave so I went in with him.

She had him on the ratty couch in her living room and she poured us both some 7 Up with a little whiskey in it. Denny sang her a few songs, and I got a little restless, and went into her kitchen while she was mooning over him. Being an enterprising guy, I looked in the cabinet below the open bottle of whiskey and saw several unopened ones. Without thinking much about it (I'd been trained with my parents' and Matt's parents' liquor holdings), I grabbed a fifth and put it under my jacket. I walked back in and said that we had to go, and Diane reluctantly peeled herself away from gazing at Denny while he played, and we left.

Considering what shape Diane was in, it was undoubtedly an irrational play for me to take a bottle of her cheap, gut-rotting rotgut, but I'd never had a bottle of cheap rotgut, and now I did. This was a victory, and my goodness, did we make the most of it.

I kept the bottle up in my closet, and some days later, Matt, Zack and I had a plan: it was probably a weekend afternoon heading into evening; we met in the yard of Matt's neighbors, a distant relative, across the street, who were out of town. They had a big treehouse in their yard, pretty nicely done, for the kid that lived there, a boy younger than us who we didn't hang out with. But with the family out of town, the treehouse was ours. And so was the whiskey.

We had some kind of soft drinks in big plastic containers, probably no ice, and a bottle of dubious whiskey. But we had enthusiasm. One of us had brought plastic glasses and so we set in with the bottle. At this point, we'd all been a bit tipsy before off of various borrowed boozes, but we'd never gotten plastered. Plastering there was, and it was successful. It was getting dark, but the treehouse was wired, though with only one plug. One of us had a cassette deck or a radio that needed a plug, but we wanted the one lamp in the treehouse to work as well.

Matt, who had sampled a goodly amount of Diane's brew, came up with an ingenious solution: we needed a three-way plug, to give our one treehouse outlet expanded electrical life. Where could such plug be obtained? Why, across the street, at Matt's house. All of us went tramping in, and Zack and I watched as Matt went through some kitchen drawers looking for the plug. When Matt's mom came into the kitchen, she asked what was up. "I want a three-way plug," Matt declared. Zack and I probably nodded in concert. But Matt's discerning mom, probably noting his glassy eyes and wobbly speech, asked, "Matt, are you all right?"

Matt was on a mission, and wasn't to be deterred. "I want a three-way plug," he insisted. His mother came a little closer, and the jig was up, probably because we reeked. She told us boys to go home, but I'm fairly sure Matt got in another plea for the plug, but to no avail. He did fess up at some point, someone went up in the treehouse and collected the evidence of our debauchery, and we didn't go to Matt's for a bit. We were lucky it was only his mom that caught us—his father would have probably tied us up and left us overnight in the garage to teach us a lesson.

To this day, any mention of a three-way plug cannot but bring a smile. And the liquor thieving? Oh my, that little taste was only the beginning. But before accumulating an impressive stash of horrible liquor (Blueberry schnapps? Just say no), many other shoplifting structures had to come into place. And perhaps a romantic humiliation or two.

I've mentioned that my family was bedrock middle-class, living in the suburbs with the trim lawns, the houses with tricycles in the yard, the family dogs. I've speculated to myself many a time (and will speculate on motivation here) why I might have turned to petty crime when I wasn't deprived of anything as a kid.

So, for this exercise, let's blame it on the suburbs and their vanilla flavorings. We'll assign other rationales later.

But I lived in a big city, now with 500,000 people—it wasn't all suburbs. Long Beach was a sailor's town, home to a now-closed naval shipyard and one of the busiest shipping ports in the U.S. There were other military influences, with plane manufacturer McDonnell-Douglas building planes, including the B-17, in the 1940s for the war effort. I am a result of one of those military exercises: my father Bob "Sarge B" Bentley was stationed just north of Long Beach in San Pedro in the 40s before he flew off as a waist-gunner in one of those B-17s, and amazingly, after so many missions—35—he flew back.

After those sorties, he met and married my mother, the lovely Eileen O'Brien out of tiny Belle Plaine, Iowa. And here we were in our suburban home in Long Beach (in those war years also called "Iowa by the Sea" because so many Iowans—including my mother and two of her sisters—made their way there). But if the suburbs were a blueprint of consistency and blandness, downtown Long Beach wasn't.

Downtown Long Beach had many things, but for us suburban kids wanting a walk on the wild side, it had the Pike.

Originally created in the 1880s as a diversion for the smart set of the time, by the 1960s its periodic facelifts could no longer hide its age. It was a motley clump of Skee-Ball houses, pinball arcades, guess-your-weight booths, and penny pitches for glum goldfish sure to be dead of pessimism by the time any dubious winners packed them home.

There was a host of tired rides, low-life bars serving up seven a.m. eye-openers, and tattoo parlors, in one of which I once saw, to my mesmerized gratification, a young woman nonchalantly getting her breast tattooed by a gnome-like sneeze of a man who intently cupped her jiggling gland while he blazed away with his buzzing gun. And who needed dangerous drugs when you could eat blue cotton candy?

This was no sunny Pacific Ocean Park (POP), the cleaner, more upscale version in Santa Monica. The Pike had the Cyclone Racer, a rickety, clattering old wooden roller coaster whose warped wheels had claimed several lives. In the mid-70s, someone discovered that a cobwebbed dummy cowboy that had lined the tracks of a Wild West ride for years was actually a desiccated victim of an unsolved shooting—discovered after the old sod was being dusted and his actual ossified arm fell off his actual human body.

Servings of apocryphal history such as these whetted the appetite for gore in my fundamental teenage constitution. The Pike had everything: it was sleazy, which was good; dangerous, which was better; and forbidden, which was delicious. You went to POP with your parents; you went to the Pike with your cronies.

Or with bad girls. Zack and I took our murky understanding of sexual matters one step further toward utter confusion when we ditched school one afternoon and went downtown. There was no uncertain glory in the thrilling randomness of wandering through downtown streets knowing that your chums were clamped to their desks.

Zack and I naturally gravitated to the Pike. We were in one of the arcade parlors playing that game that drops a tiny crane on piles of cheap toys; we were trying to use a clotheshanger wire to snag something on, up and through the prize chute.

We were fiddling with the hanger and watching for employees when we heard a smoky female voice say, "You clowns are never going to rip off that machine with that stupid wire." The voice belonged to Lynnette, maybe a couple of chronological years older than Zack and me, perhaps twenty-five years further along in worldly ways. Like the Pike, Lynnette was gaudily attractive and surely dangerous.

Her make-up looked like it had been applied with a garden trowel, and her low-cut top did little to conceal the fact that she had actual—actually momentous—breasts. At that time, I knew as much about breasts as I did about French cooking—Victoria's Secret catalogs hadn't been invented yet. Those breasts were beacons of promise for little boys who hadn't glimpsed the Promised Land.

It took all of 10 minutes of desultory conversation to establish that we were helpless slaves to her every whim. Fifteen more minutes found her in possession of some truly tacky jewelry that we stole for her upon request from one of the Pike stores specializing in second-rate adornments. Her manner and her speech matched her taste: more Wheaties than Tiffany. But her every word (many of them profane) was enough to make our hearts—and associated organs—flutter.

For the next few months the temptations of the Pike and Lynnette were wed, as Zack and I fell all over ourselves in our fumbling attempts to be wicked. We desperately vied to be the one to sit next to her on the Cyclone Racer and other rides, particularly the ones that slid us through darkened passages, prayerfully wishing that a shake or shimmy of the track might jostle us against her endlessly discussed chest. How easy was dissembling and betrayal between best friends who begged God to create weekend obligations leaving the other at home, so the free soul could pursue Lynnette —and sin(nette).

Unfortunately, the civic leaders didn't assign our worldly educations as much priority as they did to the much-vaunted Long Beach revival. The Pike, with its chipped paint and seedy reputation, had fallen into disfavor—what had been benign neglect turned into active opposition. Like so many beachside amusement parks, the Pike had glory days, rising like a Phoenix from periodic downturns, but time and chance—and a lousy profit margin—made their inexorable final claim. We were there in 1969, when the Pike's fortunes were taking a turn toward a final roller-coaster ride, but it didn't breathe its very last until the late 70s.

As for Lynnette, Zack and I went to visit her one day at her mom's house and a big dude with a shaggy mustache and not much else on answered the door and said she wasn't home, though I was certain I had heard her yelping or something a moment before. She had taught us enough about things so that we knew he wasn't the milkman. We graciously decided to spare his life, and we never saw her again.

And sadly, I wasn't to see Zack again for a couple of years: his professor pop had been offered a job at Simon Fraser University in Vancouver, so his family put some miles and a border between us. There would be some escapades on the other side of that border for Zack and I to come, but that was a ways into the future. First, I had to get better at shoplifting.

For that I needed to go to school. The shoplifting school was my own, but I also made it to a new high school as well.

CHAPTER FOUR

American Enterprise, Fingers Tingling

Kurt Vonnegut once said, "True terror is to wake up one morning and discover that your high school class is running the country." Alas, in looking at the current short-sighted, petty gyrations of our politicians, "terror" doesn't quite capture the dystopian menace. But I want to use Mr. Vonnegut's subtext here to illustrate some thoughts about characters in your stories and tales.

High school was a yeasty time: a time of turbulent yearnings, of bad complexions, of emotional cliffs, of hormonal bombardments. Enemies were defined and reviled, friends formed and clung to, selves agitated and supplanted. An overheard compliment might make you Zeus for a day, but a single smirk the next would fling you to some dark hall of Hades.

Terrifying as those times were, their living imprint aligns with Vonnegut's terror. I'd be inflating my status to say I was a real rebel in high school, but I had my moments. I'll get a little ahead of the chronology of our tale here by telling you that as much as I could, in my 16th and 17th years, I went barefoot. And that meant almost always. It was a minor creed of mine not to wear shoes—I melted at the poetry of the "If you wear shoes, the earth is covered with shoe leather" quote.

At that point, I was reading elementary Zen Buddhist books, and from popularizers of that discipline like Alan Watts, which discussed simplicity of thought and body. Throw in the budding hippie culture that greatly influenced me, and the beach culture of Southern California, and you had a guy who could often do without shoes, and chose to do so more and more often. Jesus doffed his sandals now and then, didn't he?

I always brought a pair of shoes to school, but I just carried them around, until one of the school's officers (the "narcs") would command me to put them on. Out of narc sight, I'd immediately take them off, which I did in class as well. At 17, I proudly hitchhiked from Seattle to LA barefoot. I only put on shoes when a family guy who picked me up in his RV was horrified by my feet and insisted that I take a pair of his kids' size 9 shoes to wear when he left me off. My size 13 feet had an argument with that.

My feet, as you might imagine, were pieces of work. Leathery pieces.

But at 15, entering public high school for the first time was a bit intimidating. After all, there were no longer any Catholic brothers in robes lecturing on Homer's *Odyssey*, but the full range of types (though mostly white they were) behind the teacher's desks. My new high school, Millikan, was just a skip away from St. Joseph's, my old grammar school, so I could ride my bike there or even walk.

We are such absorbent sponges in high school: I was influenced as much by Hermann Hesse as I was by Carlos Castaneda. Touched by the Grateful Dead as much as by my love of an aged Willie Mays. Entranced by language, but too lazy to do more than languidly admire its possibilities and scratch out some desultory bad verse.

The school was large, with over 3,500 students, set on the edge of the suburbs, with a decent academic reputation. I was in the incoming sophomore class while brother Rick and one of his good friends, Marty, were in their senior years there.

My brother Rick and I shared a few things, including our friends. We also, being close to the same size, shared some clothing. We traded off the wearing of a heavy, fringed leather coat that had been given to us by a friend, sometimes arguing about who got it when. We also sometimes shared the items that that coat enabled me to conceal from nosy store clerks. That coat was just a stepping stone to one of my only master tailor's acts that enabled an escalation in my pilfering. That became critical later on.

Let's mix a little liquor into the bigger equation. When I was an adolescent, I saw—demonstrated by my parents' happy application—that spirits were a lively lubricant for genial discussion and fine times. As mentioned, my parents' cabinet only seem to hold the blandest assemblage of generics. We come to our drinking habits and affections through varied paths. That mine started with theft shouldn't alarm: whiskey has a way of stealing our hearts right back

I mentioned that dusty bottle of Pinch that we sampled from Matt's father's liquor cabinet. Since Pinch bottles were too large and ungainly to slip under a jacket, I chose half-pints of Cutty Sark to steal. (At 15, what I knew of sophistication could have been inscribed on an aspirin. Scotch is Scotch, right?) Certainly, they *all* had to be spirits of distinction. Having had a Scotch as my first whisky, and not knowing the damnedest between blended Scotches or single-malts, I decided I was a Scotch drinker. It's possible Marty nudged me further in that direction, since he liked Scotch too.

To top it all, the initial larcenies were done at the scene of my original crime, the liquor store where I was the vaunted Candy Man (later the Pornography Man, begetting the Liquor Man).

It turns out that half-pint bottles were a perfect size to slip under the arm that's under a coat: easy to maneuver in, and easy to clench with your arm held down at your side. Thus, I was a Cutty Sark man for a while (and by application, a thief). I let friends outside my immediate circle know that I drank Cutty Sark. I could chalk up the fact that they weren't impressed to their ignorance. A bit later, I said I drank Famous Grouse too, because I liked the label.

My Scotch façade persisted for a period, but that didn't mean there weren't a lot of experiments—and the high-proof, what-were-we-drinking, godawful taste-science got even weirder when I left my parents' home. But in those early days, I branched out to bottles, mostly stolen from my reliable old liquor store, of some of the most miserable "wine" ever to defy the word: Ripple, Thunderbird, MD (the old Mad Dog) 20/20. They were varying degrees of foulness, but they had one thing in common: they were sweet. My sugar lust hadn't left me.

There's a gestation period for neophyte drinking and those early stages were hard on the tastebuds. We couldn't legally buy booze, and pimping it in front of liquor stores was dangerous, and got old quickly. Of course, I couldn't legally steal booze either, but after I discovered my talent for the trade, I dismissed that as a mere technicality.

One of my most interesting lessons in theft happened in this period. I was in a Woolworth's department store at our local shopping center, just browsing. I loved dinosaurs as a kid, and was in a kids' section, where they had a number of hard rubber dinosaurs about a foot tall. I'd looked at a few, and had a T-rex in my hand while I wandered through the store. I hadn't planned to buy it, but I held it while I looked at other goods and then I walked out with it still in my hand.

I didn't intend to steal it. I was immediately alarmed, looking around, heart beating. I walked back into the store and set it with the others in its bin and walked out, and again, no cashier or store employee batted an eye. I puzzled over this for a bit, and then realized that brazenness might be one of the components of good shoplifting. That there could be a time for stealth and a time for attitude: if you breezed in and breezed out, casual and composed, you could get away with things. Sometimes.

That peculiar incident became a model that proved true on a number of occasions, some of them nearly unbelievable, as you'll see. But I believed, and that was key.

That shopping center that housed the Woolworth's, a 10-minute bike ride from my house, proved to be a crucible for a number of my maturing criminal talents, and an incident during this journeyman period set off a cascade of other delinquent events, propelled by my newly stroked ego.

The shopping center had a cluster of other stores: housewares, a music store, a J.C. Penney, and a Save-on Drugs across the parking lot. But its anchor was the big The Broadway department store.

For us teenagers, The Broadway was the fancy store, with the dolled-up mannequins, the jewelry in glass cases, the racks of expensive—to us—clothes. In reality, it was a mid-tier store, but there was no Bloomingdale's in the neighborhood, and the semi-hushed atmosphere of The Broadway always made small groups of teenagers feel a bit conspicuous there.

But not so conspicuous that I couldn't steal something. Though it might be the case our mothers shopped more than us in The Broadway, we did go there occasionally because it was in that cluster of local shops we used to ramble through, even if none of us would ever buy a Burberry coat. I noticed on one of these trips, set on a tiered set of shelves that had a couple of dummies wearing men's suits (and a display of folded dress shirts, some ties, socks, perhaps shoes), was a gleaming acrylic cube that had a bunch of glinting Lincoln-head pennies set it an aligned row pattern, top to bottom.

This was a square, heavy item, six or more inches to a side, and which might have weighed a pound or more. When I picked it up from the display, I wanted it. I was with at least two other people, perhaps my brother and his friend Marty. We all hefted the cube and then set it back. When we left the store, I said I'd like to steal the cube and one of my companions said something like "No chance."

But I liked my chances. This was an opportunity to test my new personal theory of conspicuous consumption: walk in, pick up something, walk out with it, without attempting to conceal it. Now, I did many stupid things as a kid, and stealing that cube was one, but I wasn't so stupid as to think that The Broadway didn't have security in the store, and probably of the plain-clothes kind. I went back some days not long after seeing the cube, and from a distance, scoped the premises around the display. I guessed all the shoppers were civilians, and I guessed right: I walked out with the cube, scared but triumphant.

The admiring exclamations of "Wow, really?" and "Shit, you did it!" gave me a thrill of delight. I could impress my peers with my daring and prowess. That ego-clap was enough to set me deeper into the dark plunderer's forest, and I wouldn't come out without some rips in that ego, but that was to come. Getting confirmation from my peers that I had skills in something warmed me up. Granted, those skills were admittedly anti-social.

In the meantime, my wanderings in The Broadway became a bit less random. I started to check it and other venues more closely, to see what possibilities for snatchings there were. I started to consider exit locations, who might be plain-clothes people, and how those mirrored security boxes high on some store walls actually worked.

But before I tell you how my shoplifting took an upward tack as I moved from age 15 to 16, let me tell you a little bit more about the near-human I was of those days. There, my first year of public high school, I looked like (and mostly was) a classic dweeb. I was skinny, wore heavy glasses and had un-ruly hair. I had no real sense of personal style (guilty yet today) and was shy and nervous around girls.

However, I had a couple of things going for me. I was good at sports. Not great, never a star, but solid. I could play a credible game of basketball, a credible game of baseball. Never a big football fan (and not particularly strong), I could still throw and catch and run there too, though I wasn't what you'd call speedy. My father had been his high school team's quar-terback, and he played casual baseball, basketball and football with my brother and me, and encouraged us to play on teams, which we did.

My brother, two years older than me, was a better base-ball player, an All-Star pitcher in Little League. He and I used to play basketball for hours in the backyard, and pitch and hit against each other for long sessions with a tennis ball against our back gate.

Being decent at sports means that you have friends, even if they aren't real buddies. You have people to goof around with after games, people you nod to on campus. I was on the basketball team (though a sub) at my Catholic high school, and would have tried out for Millikan's squad, but I didn't—marijuana intervened, which I'll get into a bit later. But I always enthusiastically played whatever game was going in gym classes, and was comfortable there, as well as often playing whatever seasonal sport was happening on weekends with friends at pickup games.

The other advantage I had was that I loved to read. I'd watched my mother enjoy reading books for years. She used to read a lot of fiction, though not the classics, more like big historical novels and whatever came out in Reader's Digest Condensed Books. My mother took me to the local library—just across the street from the Los Altos Center of The Broadway and more—countless times between age 7–10, and I went countless more times after that, checking out the maximum number of books or just sitting in the aisles, reading.

The reason I'd picked up that rubber T-Rex in the Woolworth's? Because at eight years old I'd read every kids' dinosaur book they had in that library.

My father wasn't a real book reader, but always read the paper and magazines that came to the house. Reading seemed normal and good, and when I got into it, better than good.

So, I loved the power of words, and words themselves. I won a "Best Writer" award in eighth grade for an account of nearly drowning at a local pier. By that time in high school, I'd tried writing some goofy short stories and poems and diary-like entries. Loving words and trying to parse their meanings and their play meant that some classes that were reading-heavy, like History and English, came easily to me. Math was another story, but I could at least skate by. So, teachers generally liked me, my parents generally liked me, and I had enough friends from sports and goofing around to feel not totally alienated.

Yet the dweebish, awkward, uncomfortable side of me still wanted to impress people with something, something other than my decent jump shot or a 95 on a test. I had some anxiety issues during that period too. Well, during that period and every period afterward. Spending a great deal of time in your head is often the worst location for neutral positioning: ruminating, for me at least, often leads to chewing a bitter cud.

For a while, I was convinced that my hair was falling out, even to the point of buying a hairbrush that had bristles with no bristle: brushing my hair with that was like stroking it with a slightly damp paper towel. I would wash my hair and look at the small clump in the shower drain and recoil. Somewhere in this time I had recurring stomach pain, enough to see a doc who told my parents I had a mild stomach ulcer, for which I took some pills for a while. Damn things weren't even sugar-coated.

So, in the echo chamber of my adolescent head, I was likely more tender than necessary, even with some good stuff going for me. I needed to expand my options, look for new outlets for my talents, something new. For me, that thing turned out to be stealing things.

Practice makes perfect. So, I started practicing a little more. At 15, I wasn't stealing something every day, and might go for a couple of weeks without, but the urge would return. As well as my interest to up my game. There was another shopping center across the big street from Los Altos Center, and it was anchored by a big store called Unimart. They were discount retailers, but carried a wide range of goods, from furniture to housewares to hardware and many minor categories in between. They also carried sporting goods.

At that time, for some products the store used price tags that were attached by a little string to the product, as well as stickered tags. (This was long before the bar codes on today's goods.) I found that going up and buying something at the counter could be a good deal—particularly if you'd switched the price tag of something you were buying with something substantially cheaper. Naturally, you had to be careful with the switch—you couldn't tag an electric razor with a $1.99 price tag.

But you actually could, if you bought a number of small goods (candy, say, plus some baseball cards and comic books) along with a couple of larger ones, like a couple of baseball gloves, and brought that bounty to a counter with an older woman checker, who might not know that a $25.00 baseball glove couldn't possibly go for $4.00.

I know that sounds sexist, and it is, but when my brother and I brought a bunch of things to the counter, gloves included, the mature woman behind the register didn't bat an eye at our bargain gloves. In 1969, a $25.00–$30.00 glove from a discount store was a good one—we'd probably chosen a Rawlings or a Wilson or a Spaulding—and particularly good for a switched-tag $4.00.

Another approach was to peel off the adhesive sticker from a lower-priced item and stick it back over the true sticker price. I used that method in Unimart (which became a Two Guys and then later a Target) a number of times, as well as in other stores. I never had a problem at a register, and that gave me practice in acting like any blithe shopper: if I was shopping with a friend at the time, talking to that companion, ostensibly not paying attention to the ringing up of the ill-gotten wares was part of the game.

At this point, I thought things were going pretty well for me as a thief. I'd done a couple of daring acts, I'd refined my techniques, I'd received attention from my friends. So, for a dweeby guy, I was cultivating a roguish side. I felt daring. But I was a rank amateur in the crimes count when compared to some of our other friends. Next door to us lived Steve, a kid my age who was also Denny's cousin. He lived with his mom, stepfather and stepsisters.

His father, a former Marine, was a crazy guy, an engaging storyteller when sober—which wasn't often—and a mean drunk when he wasn't. He once slapped Steve hard across the face for sneezing at the table when we were eating lunch together.

I've told you that we used to run around a lot as kids in the neighborhood. We did the usual kid stuff, knocking on doors in the evenings and hiding in nearby bushes to see the exasperated homeowners open the door to an empty step. The first time Steve went out knocking on doors with us, he bashed some person's door with a baseball bat he was carrying. Another time he lit a car on fire. I wasn't there, but many people testified to the truth of the tale. We didn't ask Steve to come out knocking on doors with us after that. Even though he was a good guy, he seemed to carry some built-up hostility, maybe from the abuse his father showered on him.

I'm not sure where the motivations of Steve's cousin Chet (who didn't live in our neighborhood, but close) originated, but he was a creative demon. I was taking small pride in snatching things out of stores without being caught, no guilt pangs involved. That was nothing. I was legitimately paying for something at a store counter with Chet when he took the March of Dimes donation box off the counter and put it under his shirt. My Catholic upbringing told me the flames of hell would patiently wait for Chet's arrival.

But while they waited, Chet continued his work. We were at a local gas station once, together at the outside Coke machine. He stopped me from paying. Where he'd gotten it, I'll never know, but he had one of those round-shafted cylinder keys for the machine. Not only did we get free Cokes, he poured half of the contents of the coin box into his pockets, with nary a gas station attendant in the know.

On another occasion, I was riding with him on the back of his old Honda 160 at a traffic signal behind a beer delivery truck. He jumped off the bike, shocking me by telling me to hold the motorcycle up, and he ran to the back of the truck, cranked open the big slot lock on the big doors, grabbed a case of beer and closed up the truck quickly enough to bring the case back to me on the bike before the truck roared away. He pulled over and strapped that case to the bike (and against me) and he struggled back home—who knows where he hid it.

Chet was a true original. Perhaps a year later, he'd bought an old Chevy that he'd rigged up with a very loud "Ooo-ugah" horn that he operated by pulling a string under the dash. When he saw a girl on the street he liked, he'd pull that thing with gusto. The car had a fancy custom steering wheel, a tiny little chrome thing that once came off in his hands, while driving, while several of us were in the car. Chet just laughed and slapped it back on.

So yes, I was a minor criminal, but I could always say I was never as bad as Chet or Steve. Not at that point, at least. But their exploits did inspire.

I considered all my wiles I learned over time when I was a little lad, when I used to plaintively cry to my mom a half-hour before I had to leave for school that I had a stomachache, or a headache or I didn't feel well. Those dramatics would be accompanied by my squinched-up, pained grimace face and clutching of the allegedly ailing body part—an act that she would only buy one out of ten times. I brought all that to mind and tried again on a Sunday when most of the whole family was going to church, like we did together for years.

For some reason, they'd taken my father's old Ford sedan, rather than the big Ford station wagon we owned as well. (My father worked at Ford for all those years, thus, we were a Ford family.) Mass only lasted an hour or so, so my excursion would be brief. I thought I'd steal the sedan but the station wagon it was. From having stolen my father's change over the years, I knew the keys would be in the same area, the old brown ceramic bowl up in the kitchen cupboard.

I was glad the wagon was on the street, because I wouldn't have to back out of our narrow driveway that flanked the house. I turned it over, it started and I was off. Now, I'd taken driver training at school, and had driven a car with an instructor a couple of times. In fact, I'd been the astonished (and gratified) passenger in a driver-training car when one of my fellow students, who could not have been five feet tall and who could barely see over the wheel, attempted a Y-turn in the driveway of a house in a suburban neighborhood, and when she was supposed to back out, she was still in Drive, and before the instructor could react, literally drove into the closed garage door and smashed it. She became famous.

I went out onto the big boulevard that was perpendicular to our street, and headed up toward the liquor store that was— and would remain—one of the mainstays of my early thieving. But I wasn't going to stop for anything—this was strictly a joyride. But I had no joy, because I was a crappy driver, I was nervous as a leaf in the wind, and I was driving a giant American station wagon, badly.

I turned at a traffic signal and was driving parallel to a long drainage ditch when I took my eye off the straight and narrow (probably staring wide-eyed looking for cops in the rear-view mirror) and hit the curb that separated cars from the ditch and started to go up on the curve into the ditch. This ditch, probably four or five feet deep with steep slanted walls, was where my friend Zack and I had watched a car crash into and out some time before, with it landing upside-down on the other side of the ditch on the residential street that paralleled it.

That ditch.

But I didn't go over and in. I wrenched the car to the left, it lurched back into the lane, and for some reason my heart didn't stop completely. My joyride that never was, was over. I headed home as soberly as I could, parked the car carefully where it had been parked, with no neighbor seeing, and went back in the house in plenty of time to sit and imagine my ditch death over and over.

That was probably enough reason not to steal my parents' car again, but the next time I did it, I had a license. That must have made it OK, right? But those car-klepto escapades came much later—there was a lot of calamity in between.

CHAPTER FIVE

Don't Do This at Home (or at School)

Since we were a family of six, most of the time I wasn't home alone, except for those holy occasions where I'd faked illness, or by some other strange confluence of events. But when I was 15 getting on 16, my brother started working at my mom's restaurant, where both my older sisters worked part-time as well, and my dad didn't come home until after 5, so I occasionally found myself with a couple of hours alone at home.

Did I vacuum or garden or take up a charity collection around the neighborhood? Not exactly. What I sometimes did was go through all the drawers in the house, to see what secrets they might hold. Thus I found a carefully rolled joint in one of my sister's jewelry boxes, what looked like a Seconal pill in another. I found that my brother had a big coffee can for his tips at work hidden in the furnace cabinet. I found that my parents had an envelope taped to the back of their dresser that held cash.

Did I smoke the joint, take the pills, or steal the envelope's cash? No. However, I did steal change from my brother's can occasionally, and probably just for when I didn't feel like stealing candy. What are brothers for? At that point, my brother had a Honda 90 motorcycle that he occasionally let me ride. However, sometimes when he wasn't home, he occasionally didn't let me ride it, but I rode it anyway. He discovered that by having recorded the mileage on the odometer—and I was chastised.

Once he established that stratagem, I parried it by unscrewing the odometer cable and riding the bike, without any mileage giveaway. I barely rode it for more than 15 minutes at a time, but, if you've been paying attention, you might have noticed that I liked getting away with things. My brother and my friends also paid attention to when the neighbors on either side of us weren't home too, and when we knew it was clear, we snuck into their houses and went through their drawers as well. I'd had practice, so I knew the technique. We never took anything from their houses, but a violation of propriety (and property) it surely was.

My 15th year was a cultural escalation, for America and for me. In 1969, the Vietnam War raged, and many of my California high school buddies raged with it. None of us were particularly savvy politically, but there seemed to be a pointless injustice to it, our fighting the damn Commies, without much in the way of a victory, a million miles away, under Nixon's helm. The peace sign was our sign too.

That was also a year of great music: the Stones, the Beatles, Dylan, Neil Young, Marvin Gaye—the list could go on and on. Woodstock was coming in the summer ahead. But I had only a few albums, a cheap record player and no cassette player. I listened to the pop and rock stations whenever I could, but I coveted playing albums at home. There was a vast divide between my allowance and the purchasing of electronic devices. But that divide could be narrowed if those items came to me by virtue of magic. Er, I mean stealing.

At that point, I was fairly good with going into stores and stealing small things. I managed to get half-pints of liquor out of our local store without too much trouble, though I was still nervous about it, and heaved sighs of relief when I got out of the store unfollowed. But my fear didn't stop me from trying to pilfer new things. I mentioned that going to the counter to buy items with switched tags was a decent ruse. It was also a cover for having something up your sleeve while you paid for something trivial at the counter.

One method was to wear a long-sleeved coat and hold something long and flat against the inside of your wrist and forearm, clamping the item and sleeve down with pressure from your fingers on the outside of the coat. I'd keep that occupied arm down my side and pay for something with the other hand. I got so that I could bring something up to the counter and steal some promotional items—pens, toy baseball bats, card decks, goofy gifts, countertop tchotchkes of sleeve shape—while I was paying, right under the nose of the cashier, which gave me that little ego kick of getting away with something I loved so well.

I had continued to use the heavy, fringed-leather coat shared by my brother and me as my pilfering coat, but it was a little out of place in Southern California warmth, even for a tangled-haired kid in the late 60s. (Though it did work well for stealing boxes of incense out of our local head shop, plus a matching fringe leather belt, which was undoubtedly a violation of the Summer of Love.)

But I also had my "classy" coat, which to that point I hadn't been using for my handiwork. The reason I called it my classy coat was that it was blazer-style, though of dimly green corduroy and fairly wide lapels. Not something that you'd see a dignitary wearing at a Lions Club presentation for most money raised at a car wash, but to me, my formalwear.

Another reason it was classy was that it was a coat I wore (or tried to be wearing) when I smoked the wretchedly bad cigars Zack and I stole from, you guessed it, the local liquor store. Being a true sophisticate, I equated cigar smoking with grace and style, so I used to steal almost hallucinatorily bad cigars: blueberry flavored Tiparillos, Swisher Sweets, and other cigars dosed with horrid sweetly artificial flavors (note my traditional sugar urge here).

The Tiparillos had the characteristic plastic tip, out of which would drip vile sweet/sour colored juices—death cherry, anyone?—when you got to the end of the stogie. And because we understood that wine drinking was classy too, we magnified our man-about-town efforts by stealing some of my parents' wine when we'd go and hide somewhere in the neighborhood (and even in my backyard) and smoke those things and drink the wine. Since my parents bought Gallo by the gallon and mystical things like Tawny Port, we matched the quality of the cigars with that of the wine.

But we were classy, by God.

Besides class, the coat had other potentials too. It was broad-shouldered, loose and light, and hung down well past the tops of my pockets. I had been trying to work out how I could steal a cassette player under the heavy fringe jacket, but it was too bunched-up at my shoulders. I also didn't know how I could keep something as heavy as a cassette player underneath my coat without dropping it or obviously carrying something underneath.

The corduroy coat and a new approach solved the problem. I practiced in front of a mirror at home with slipping a semi-bulky square object under my coat and carrying it. With something heavy, that wasn't easy to do with my arm held at my side because I couldn't grip the item in my armpit with the right strength to easily carry it out of the store, and something with square edges, even with that loose coat, visibly pushed the shoulder of the coat up and out, both front and back.

I struggled with that, eyeing my front and back in the mirror with something held under my arm, and not liking the results. But then it came to me: if I held something in my hands, so that my arm was out in front, perpendicular to my body, I could not only put more pressure on the object, but because the coat would billow up more naturally with my arm up, the telltale "what's that guy got in his coat" dents weren't as obvious.

The key: pretending to need to clean my glasses, either with a handkerchief or the edge of my t-shirt (which I wore under that coat almost always—classy, right?). In that position, both hands raised in front of my chest while cleaning my glasses, I could hold the pilfered thing more tightly, and conceal it better.

And, also appear a little bit pathetic: look, that kid has to clean his glasses and walk at the same time, the poor thing.

This technique probably sounds like pure idiocy, and it probably was, but it worked. I tested it with some smaller things at stores, not as bulky as that day's style of portable cassette players, but as proof-of-concept. Then I went after the real thing.

That big Unimart store I mentioned in the scene about switching baseball glove price tags was still there, but it had become a Two Guys store. Whatever corporate cash-counters behind Two Guys made this decision, I thank you. Not because the store changed at all—or not that me at 15 could tell how it changed, other than the sign, but because they'd still let me in the doors.

And behind those doors was a fairly big electronics section, with large console-style home stereos, home 8-track players (ahh, those were the days), boom boxes, and portable cassette players, my designated prey. If I recall correctly, Unimart/Two Guys did have some of those two-way mirror boxes high on what I presumed were its second-story office walls, but there weren't a lot of them, and who knows if there was anyone back there looking.

This was long before today's ubiquitous unmanned camera setups or electronic tags. Many stores wouldn't have wanted to waste an employee sitting for hours behind one of those wall mirrors, but perhaps they did do stints behind them. But even then, like in many large department stores, aisles were often crowded with goods and high shelves, so that many areas of a big store were concealed from even a high eye.

I can't recall how many times I walked around the electronics area, checking out the cashier, other shoppers, shoppers in the specific vicinity, and my own beating heart. I do remember it was daytime, so it had to be on a weekend. I also remember the cassette players were on a tilted shelf, so that their beckoning face addressed shoppers. And again, security was loose then: no cables or other attachments to secure the device to the shelf.

I was checking out the players, of which there were several, and then picked up one in my right hand while I slipped the one in my left hand under my jacketed right arm, which was raised to give better access. I set down the other and walked, cleaning my glasses all the while, probably sweating, out of the store, out on to the sidewalk, and into a deeper channel of my business enterprise.

The tape player was a Panasonic, one of the premier manufacturers of cassette players then, a black-and-silver gleaming thing, and quite mine. I had a few cassettes at home, and already had batteries: sweet. And the sound that came out of the thing also seemed sweet to my non-audiophile ears. I did have to hide it, but not from my brother, who at that point was more aware of my work. Bulky, but not so that it couldn't go behind or under some other closet items.

The thing about stolen cassette players? You could steal the tapes to play in them as well. They were small and very easy—I could even do the nothing-down-my-sleeve trick with them. Some music stores kept their cassettes in locked, see-through cases that you could swing around for look-but-don't-touch, but many, like the larger department stores, just had them out and available, and many were simply wrapped in cellophane, so no bulky box.

It would take a while for the idea to crystalize, but the crystals soon lined up: if I could steal one cassette player, I could steal more. And somebody at school would probably pay for it. That supposition was proven true after I'd had the cassette player at home for a bit and decided to take it to school. There was no plausible reason to do this other than to show off. Busted.

Steppenwolf had released their "Born to Be Wild" album the year before, and the title song was a hit I liked. After all, I was raised in the suburbs—wild, no? I stole that cassette out of a music store, and had been playing it a lot in my room.

There was a beautiful, very tall, very smart girl in one of my classes, might have been History, that usually sat opposite me, close to the back of the room. Her name was Merrilee, and we were friendly in class, but not friends. In my insightful way, I guessed that playing "The Pusher" from that Steppenwolf album in class, low, but not so low she couldn't hear the lyrics, would be helpful, particularly the lyrics which at one point, say,

God damn, The Pusher

God damn, I say The Pusher

I said God damn, God damn The Pusher man

Work with me here: I figured that playing daring lyrics like those next to Merrilee would likely tell her I was a pretty cool guy and that paying more attention to me would pay off. I had such confidence in this tack that I played it twice in a row. Merrilee did look over and smile a couple of times. At least she did seem to smile. Later I found out that Merrilee's boyfriend was one of the school's bigger jocks, a hulking football player nicknamed "Chewy." I needn't say more.

However, that moment impelled one of my other classmates, a guy whose name and face I can't remember, to excitedly ask me after class, "Hey, where'd you get the tape deck? That's cool!" Though I'd done some show-offish things with my friends regarding my thievery, I wasn't ready to tell an acquaintance how I'd come by the player. But when he offered, I was ready to sell it to him.

I don't recall their retail price, but I'm sure I sold it to him for $25 or $30 or so, which in 1969 was a decent amount of money for a high school lad who was jobless. My initial thought was to steal another one so I could continue to have one of my own. But that thought was supplanted: Why not steal another one and sell it? Businesses need growth, I'd heard. I didn't see myself as a businessperson yet, just a thief, but I probably sensed the two might coalesce nicely. I had to put a couple of other processes in place first.

And one of those processes was learning how to get stoned. For all those kids now smoking pot at age 9 and saying "Loser!" when they hear I began at age 15, I will say with a wry smile: yes, callow youth I was, but I accelerated from a standing stop pretty rapidly. I knew what pot was and had certainly heard of other drugs and had, as I duly noted, seen a joint in my sister's jewelry box. But I hadn't smoked any.

Lucky for me I had an older generation to lead me. Astray, that is. My older sister Colleen was a social sort, having kept a good crowd of friends from her Catholic high school days, her various jobs and her early college years. As a family, every second summer, we'd go on long trips to either Iowa (my mother's territory) or Colorado (my father's) or sometimes both. But those trips always involved a stopover in Las Vegas for a day or two.

My parents loved to gamble, mostly slots and Keno, occasionally blackjack, craps and roulette. I adopted their sustained skills at losing years later when I lived in Las Vegas, and Colleen did too. But occasionally my parents went to Vegas for a quick trip on their own. The inaugural occasion of smoking weed came when the old folks were gone and my older sister threw a daytime party at our place.

I knew a lot of my sister's friends, and they tolerated me and my brother being around more than our sisters did. One of her friends was Phil, the first gay person I'd known. Phil was handsome, with long, lustrous black hair, a loud, high voice and a sharp wit. He later figured in several adventures with me and my friends in Hollywood, where we met drag queens and attended a couple of raucous gay bars. When I was older, that is: 16. (I'll get to a couple of those jaunts in due time.)

But on this occasion, Phil brought my brother and me into our room and said he had some Acapulco Gold to smoke. Of course, with dispensaries dispensing freely now, you can buy weed with a thousand different names and strengths, whether it's dubbed Gorilla Bottom or Chariot of the Gods or Old Hubcaps, but in those days, there were only a few named types of pot, like Maui Wowee and Acapulco Gold.

He lit up a meager pinner in our room and we both took it in. I loved the smell right off the bat and the taste too— remember, I'd been smoking those Blueberry Tiparillos— though I don't remember getting particularly high (but I suppose not remembering is part of the game). I'm not sure my sister even knew he welcomed us into the club, but that threw the doors open wide.

In that period of the middle of my sophomore year to my 16th birthday, I went from that first timid taste of weed to discovering who the dealers were at school, to buying and smoking regularly with my friends, to dropping acid and taking psychedelic mushrooms. That was an education. I can't say it escalated my interest in shoplifting, but it certainly didn't make me more cautious about it.

I must confess as well to once splitting a whole can of nutmeg spread on bread with my friend Matt, because we'd read that eating a significant amount of nutmeg can get you high. Oh, it can: if you call getting high having a horrible stomach ache and bleary-eyed distress.

That didn't stop us from once eating commercially available morning glory seeds (same result as above), smoking dried coleus leaves, and trying to make lettuce-heart "opium" out of squeezed and pounded lettuce hearts (no result at all, unless you count puzzled embarrassment).

We move rapidly as kids, and often without seatbelts. That year between 15 and 16 was a "you forgot to get your brakes checked, but what the hell" year. As these pages suggest, at 16, I was a junior in high school, a nice boy who ate dinner with his parents, and a lawless deviant.

I mentioned Woodstock earlier. I fretted, fussed and plotted about Woodstock, frustrated that at 15, I didn't have the means or the gumption to get there. I had to wait to buy the albums, hear the stories and understand the significance. I had to wait a bit longer before I got to go to what some people dubbed the "West Coast Woodstock." The 1970 "Christmas Happening" in Laguna Beach didn't have the thronging masses, or the heralded music, or the dynamics to make it more than a scribble in the history books. But it was in my neighborhood.

And it did have LSD dropped from an airplane in the sky.

To wit, late in 1970 when my friends and I saw the posters circulating news about a concert in Laguna, we were stoked. Laguna Beach was only 40 miles south from my Long Beach home, but it seemed a million miles in culture. Long Beach was sprawling, paved-over, unhip; Laguna was small, had organic food stores, hippies and head shops, and a spar-kling beach. Laguna was, to our unsophisticated eyes, impressively *groovy*. Whether the event would be a Wood-stockian "three days of fun and music" or not, go we must.

The posse: me, my older brother, and two close friends. Marty, mentioned before, was probably my brother Rick's closest friend, a mentor for me, whose recommendations on provocative books and music were gold. Dennis, our old neighbor, was my age, an exuberant guy who was willing to go out further on limbs than most, but when he fell, wings sprouted so that he always landed on his feet.

Denny and Marty both had cars, and one of them drove. The murk of memory makes some details soft, but the high-lights—and my, there were some—all happened, even though some might have happened on the astral plane. But even 50 years can't erase some sharp memories of people behaving ex-ceedingly strangely.

But first, some background on the concert, much that I only found out years later.

The idea for the festival came from a guy named Curtis Reid, a Laguna local who had a number of friends in the alter-native community. Reid was the force behind getting the posters printed and getting the word out about the concert. That word moved from the local hippie communities to alter-native newspapers and radio to mainstream media. What was expressed as a celebration of Christ's birthday with love and music mushroomed into a looming event that alarmed the more conservative citizens of Laguna Beach.

Some accounts had it that the festival was originally slated for downtown's Main Beach, but the final site was Sycamore Flats, outside of town in the soft hills of Laguna Canyon. Our Christmas family gatherings prevented us from going that first day of the concert, but on the morning of Dec. 26th, we set out for the site. We had no clue that the nearby streets would be choked with cars, some left, ala Woodstock, on the sides of roads far from the festival. Woodstockers in training, we left our car on a dirt pull-out a fair distance from the canyon, and walked in.

We also had no clue that the concert was, let's say, not particularly organized. Having already hosted the first day of the concert, the site displayed a lot of Christmas wrapping, in the form of sagging tents, trash, rumpled blankets, camping equipment and backpacks. There were lots of people, certainly several thousand, probably more. Some later crowd estimates had it at 20–25 thousand, but I wonder.

We managed to maneuver somewhat near the stage and set up our blankets amid crowds of other blanketeers. Some guy on stage was flatly playing an acoustic guitar and warbling out a listless tune. We set about to smoke as much pot as possible in as short of time as possible. That's when the fun began.

A thin woman with long dark hair and a billowy hippie dress ascended the stage and in a quavering, piercing voice started to harangue the crowd. "Animals are your friends. Please don't eat the animals. Love animals, don't eat them." She repeated this as a refrain, with mild variation, over and over for long, long minutes. As chance would have it, just as she was beginning her rant, I was eating some Vienna sausages from the can.

If you've never eaten Vienna sausages (and you shouldn't), they are allegedly made of pork. But surely parts of that pork were pig snouts and hooves, and probably pig regrets and bad dreams. And enough salt to paralyze a horse. But I was 16 and high—I would have eaten anything. Despite my thick-headedness, I made a hazy association between the preachings of the woman and what I was eating. I then pushed the cans of sausages under some clothing, so none of her friends would see and drag me to the stage as an example of the Antichrist.

After her performance, a boogie-blues band came on, followed by some strident rock. At this point, I realized that part of what seemed a dentist's drill of recrimination from the stage was partially due to the sound system. Lots of screechy feedback, dropouts and inconsistent volume. This did not improve. Nor did, to my ear, the quality of the music. But we'd never conclusively heard that any big-name bands would come, so we were satisfied with the sonic sludge we were served. Allegedly Buddy Miles was there for at least one of the days, but I might have hiked out of the canyon to throw those Vienna sausage cans away and missed him.

It was only when the PA guy would periodically announce that "George Harrison has been seen in the crowd," or "David Crosby is right now in a helicopter on his way," that big cheers would go up, only to sag soon after when another unknown band crawled onto the stage. But the biggest cheers came soon afterward. I'd seen in the distance a small plane drop what look liked leaflets on the gathering. None landed right near us, but not too far either.

In the spirit of Christmas, a local organization called the Brotherhood of Eternal Love managed to drop thousands of hits of Orange Sunshine affixed to colorful cards from a small plane onto the masses. Some said hundreds of cards, others up to 25,000. The cards circulated through the crowd, and Marty and Dennis took their share. It's hard to say what is harder on your body, Orange Sunshine or Vienna sausages, but I opted out, for a strong reason.

Months before, I'd gone to a Bo Diddley concert at the Long Beach Arena with Dennis, and we'd both dropped some Orange Sunshine. I later had to flee, because my torqued mind told me that Bo was deliberately playing specific notes to torment me and me alone, and each tone sent my brain convulsing. The Arena being miles from my suburban home, we started to get on a public bus, when I had a revelation: *Money is evil!* I declared this loudly to the bus driver while we were getting in, tossed all the paper cash in my wallet on the floor, and for good measure, tossed my glasses to the floor too, because I was liberating myself of needless earthly things.

Dennis managed to retrieve some of my money and my glasses, and pulled me from the bus. We walked for *hours* to get home—lucky for us that speedy acid is like drinking a thousand cups of coffee. On a roller-coaster. Thus, at the Laguna concert, I wasn't that hungry for Orange Sunshine. My brother, never having developed an appetite for being flung out of a rainbow-colored car at 60 mph, didn't take any either.

As I only found out years later, the benevolent Brotherhood was one of the biggest distributors of acid in the U.S. They believed it was a holy sacrament. Ever-so Southern California, they occasionally smuggled drugs in hollowed-out surfboards. The Brotherhood hooked up with some skilled acid cookers, like Tim Scully, who'd been mentored by Owsley Stanley, probably the most famed of the LSD chemists. In his spare time away from solvents and reagents, Owsley also designed the Grateful Dead's famed—and titanic—Wall of Sound system. (Needless to say, this was not the sound system used at the concert.)

The Brotherhood's honorary high priest was Timothy Leary, who'd earlier been busted for pot in Laguna. The whole story is very tangled, but allegedly the Brotherhood paid thousands to later have Leary busted out of jail. Who did the deed? The infamous anarchist group, the Weather Underground. Possibly the Black Panthers also helped to smuggle him out of the country, though he was recaptured later. See how acid unites everyone?

Back at the concert, Hendrix hadn't shown up, but people were high. Very high. Perhaps fifty yards in front of me, I saw the first living, fully naked woman of my life. I thought that was delightful, until she broke away from the group she was standing with, and ran, flat-out full speed, into the side of a parked truck. That, with the horrible sound of speeding human flesh hitting immovable object, was not delightful. Some folks carted her away.

And then Marty carted Dennis away, to one of the medical tents. Denny had found himself naked and was offering spiritual counsel to some of the women nearby. Marty managed to get him into the flip-out center, where they eventually returned him to the earth, and re-clothed him, since his duds were lost in transit. Marty did report that on the way back, he saw two naked, muddy people having sex standing up. Recently, Dennis told me that in the tent he was hallucinating a choice between God and the Devil, and that he chose not to die, and to be with God. A good choice, as it turned out.

Here's where our stories diverge: Denny and Marty say we spent the night, but my brother and I are sure we went home in the evening. It's possible that we hitchhiked home and they stayed, because we hitchhiked a lot in those days, and there were lots of people leaving the concert. If we did hitchhike home, I'm thankful no acid-fueled concertgoer picked us up, thinking he was driving a dragon, or perhaps a NASA moonshot.

Regardless, despite our efforts, we survived. The concert did go on for another day (even with many police roadblocks), and a couple of thousand people stayed in the canyon until the 28th, when the Laguna and Orange County cops raided the place and forced everyone out, bulldozers blazing. Not quite the sweeping landscape of debris you see in Woodstock depictions, but the place was pretty trashed. From that point, Laguna wasn't as receptive to the hippie vibe as it had been.

Some big busts followed for the Brotherhood and its associates, and more tangled tales, like that one of their later biggest LSD manufacturers was also a CIA informant. Leary was pardoned in 1976 by Jerry Brown, our beloved Governor Moonbeam. Me, I started going to Grateful Dead concerts. I continued to take acid now and then. I kept my glasses. I stopped eating Vienna sausages. I can still spell.

I never did make it to Woodstock, but I was at the concert where acid came down from the sky. You'll have to wait for the movie.

I do regret that my burgeoning interesting in sautéing my brain with various substances drained my interest in trying to make the high school junior-varsity basketball team. I wasn't fast, and wasn't that tall (though I did leave high school at 6'1" or so, and still growing), but I probably could have made a solid benchwarmer who would have gotten into some one-sided games, and that might have been enough. I still loved sports, and played basketball and baseball (and softball) when I could, but the red-eyed kid smoking weed out behind the gym lacked full motivation.

I didn't lack motivation to improve my larceny techniques though: there was much expansion ahead.

CHAPTER SIX

Nothing Up My Sleeve

I've already described the loose corduroy coat that had transformed into a fine tool of theft. By the time I was 16, now a junior in high school, I had stolen many cassette players from the Two Guys store using that coat, my ever-perfecting armpit clamp and the cleaning-the-glasses ruse. As I mentioned, I sold them at school, along with the occasional cassette tape that came my five-fingered way as well. But those were just small forays into capitalism and the free market (which for me meant stolen things). I was open to new challenges.

That coat had a dark, satiny inner liner. As I said, it hung loosely on me, and though I was around six feet tall at that time, it hung well past my jeans pocket openings, so I could use it to conceal small, flat objects I pocketed.

Besides cassettes, I also wanted records, but there was no way I could slip a large, square album into that coat under my arm without it being conspicuous, no matter how loose it was. But I thought it over, and though no tailor, I cut with scissors across the breadth of one side of the coat's liner so that it created a broad, inner pocket, between liner and the inner coat fabric, wide enough even to slip an album in.

I checked it out from multiple angles in the mirror: yes, if I held my arm right, the coat's shape, fabric and structure (it had mild shoulder pads) concealed that there was music within. I tried it the first time at the local Sav-On drug store. Sav-On was indeed a pharmacy, but a big one, like a CVS of today, with all kinds of household goods and supplies. One of those supplies was albums and again, the aisles of these stores were often high with goods on their shelves—unless someone was in the aisle with you, it was easy to do dirty work undetected.

That process was indeed successful, helped by going to the counter and buying something, rather than just leaving the store without an obvious purchase. The first LP I corralled was "Let It Be," the last album by the Beatles, still one of my favorite bands. I ended up stealing three separate "Let It Be" records, selling a couple at school. But the album I really wanted, to keep and to sell, was the 3-disk Woodstock set, something so bulky I didn't want to risk trying to put it in that inner liner.

Such a problem. But you know what they say about necessity (and for a 16-year-old with dubious morals, necessity was an amorphous situation). The Los Altos Center, the site of so many of my formative thefts, had many stores that would bag up your purchases and seal the bag by stapling the receipt to the top of the bag, so that it was a visible sign you'd made a purchase. Almost all of them had the store's name in big letters printed on the receipt at the top; some of them, like The Broadway, had their store names printed on the bags.

I systematized my work: Making cheap purchases, I collected bags and legitimate receipts from all the major area stores. I bought a tiny stapler that I carried in one of my coat's pockets, for those stores that stapled purchases in the shut bag. At Sav-On, I bought a record, got the bag and receipt, and went home. But a few evenings later, with that bag carefully folded under my coat, I went to the record section, unfolded that bag and loaded six or seven albums in, including Woodstock, and stapled the bag shut, just like every cashier did at every Sav-On counter.

I walked out with that bag casually tucked under my arm, receipt showing. I probably also looked like I was running a fever, because this was a gambit I hadn't used before. Despite my agitation, it worked. Over some days, I sold a number of those records at school, but I did keep a Woodstock for myself. I could play that Santana solo on "Soul Sacrifice" until the needle broke.

I don't want to give the impression that I went out pillaging every night and every weekend. I was still hanging out with friends, doing some homework, playing baseball or basketball, reading. And trying to figure out how to get a girl, any girl, to like me. Besides, I wouldn't have been able to hide huge amounts of ill-begotten goods. But it was pretty easy to hide, say, 10 records and a cassette deck or smaller things, as long as I kept them circulating out of the house too, while making a small profit in the bargain. As I said, my parents trusted me: how could a nice boy like me be stealing?

I was lucky that my first instance of getting caught flat-footed (besides my candy caper) turned out to be a time that my parents weren't in town. They were gone to Las Vegas, and my oldest sister Colleen was watching us, if by watching us you mean ignoring us as best she could. One of my friends asked me to steal a particular shirt from The Broadway, the nice department store that had unknowingly donated the acrylic cube to me long months earlier.

At that point, I'd stolen a couple of shirts from there, maybe a sweater too, using the bag/receipt ploy. This time I hadn't cased the joint with careful scrutiny. A plainclothes guy stopped me outside the store, and brought me back in to a small room with the store manager and took down all kinds of identifying information about me on a form.

The two left the room, leaving me thinking they were going to call the cops. But they didn't: They called my parents' house, and Colleen answered, and since she was over 18, they said she could come down and pick me up. They came back in the room to say Colleen would be coming to get me, and to let me know that I was banned from the store, and that they would send a copy of the form to the local police.

Only they wouldn't be able to do that, because while they were out of the room, I stole the form out of the filing cabinet the plainclothes guy put it in. I was exceedingly pleased with myself for that work. Sadly, being insufferable was part of my pilferer's makeup. I also congratulated myself on my cleverness later when I dribbled a basketball out of the same department store where I'd been caught taking the home-stereo 8-track player mentioned in the introduction. The basketball was much easier to dribble.

I mentioned Zack's move to Canada before. With Zack gone, I didn't really have a shoplifting partner any longer. I think my brother and our pal Marty both did a bit of shoplifting, and probably my friend Denny too, but that effort never even became a hobby for them, much less a pursuit as it was for me.

However, Denny, with some help from me, was a temporary but enthusiastic bicycle thief for a short while, which in memory is another note that pangs me, since I was a bike rider. Why would we steal people's bicycles? But we did steal a few 10-speeds from suburban garages, and repainted them in Denny's dad's carport for resale. That was nasty, and we didn't do it more than a few times.

Even my impervious 16-year-old conscience—honestly, I had one—raised its dormant head now and then. Though my conscience had a short memory, and not a lot of energy. It was easily lulled back to sleep.

So now, I didn't have a true partner in crime. But a friend of a friend from high school, with whom I started hanging out more and more, seemed to have a real aptitude. I found that out after he'd bought a briefcase from me at school, probably a thin, very uncool-for-high-school black Samsonite, which was the first one I'd stolen. This was a classic example of "Act like you own it and you do" from the recipe of brazenness tactics.

I remarked earlier that some acts of theft can be accomplished by simply walking out of the store with the thing comfortably in your hands. (Or if it's dribble-able, dribble it out.) "Comfortably" is key here: you must behave as if everything is normal.

In 1969, my first year at public high school, there were restrictions on how long boys could wear their hair. They loosened some of those strictures in 1970, so that we could finally begin looking as scruffy as the rock stars we admired. My hair was beginning to grow out in 1970 and my beard was coming in heavier. I should say my hair was beginning to grow up, since it was unruly stuff, so that when it got actually long a year or so later, it was a quasi-Afro.

That was when my father bought my brother and I matching dresses, hung them in our closets, and said he was going to call us Gladys and Gertrude from then on. He also bought us a can of Aqua Net hairspray, the brand used by my sisters to glue their hair impossibly high off their heads, and to turn the bathroom into a toxic waste dump in the process.

My father was always a funny man, but he didn't think much of our looks or locks. My brother recently reminded me that we had a poster of a hippie-haired Jesus on our bedroom door that said, "Tell them Jesus says you can wear your hair as long as you want," but my dad didn't seem to get religion on that account.

I was focusing more on my shoplifting, but doing enough schooling to get by. On the broader scale, the U.S. was in deep (and often sour) ferment about the Vietnam War, and there were protests all over the country. The killings at Kent State didn't calm anything down. I was against the war, as were most of my friends, and as more information came out about how it was conducted, more hardened to it. But matters thousands of miles away weren't on my day-to-day.

Even though my hair in 1970 wasn't the Sasquatch look it would take on in later years, I was still unkempt looking. Not the look that went with carrying a "Man in the Grey Flannel Suit" briefcase. But there was the beauty of it. I'd noticed that briefcases in one of the other local big department stores, I believe it was a J.C. Penney, were fairly expensive. One day I walked in, and soon walked out, blithely carrying a new Samsonite. It was incongruous that the kid I was would be walking around with a briefcase, but no one said a word. Held low by the handle at my side, like I'd carried a briefcase to every class for the last two years, I became a business guru just by exiting the store.

I became more of a shoplifting guru to Tom, the friend I mentioned earlier, when I told him how I'd gotten the briefcase. He was particularly interested in the details of shoplifting, which wasn't surprising, because he was attentive to details. I'd had discussions with my brother and friends, particularly Zack before he left town, about five-finger techniques, showing them my coat, my way of holding things inconspicuously under the coat, and the innocent look with which one strolls out of a store. It was shoplifting school, but on a casual basis.

Tom was less casual (and shockingly less, as you'll read when I detail his later exploits). He was a guy who could take apart a Volkswagen engine down to the last washer and put it back together without a curse word. His parents had a big garage—but it was more like Tom's garage—where he'd take apart broken radios, electric mixers, small motors and the like and bring them to life again.

I'd never seen so many tools, and never knew a guy his age who knew how to use them. One of his things was that he'd go out on some weekends on his bike with a stack of cards that said, "Do you want to sell this car? If so, call me" with his number. He might tag 100 cars with the cards under the wipers, cars that looked like they hadn't been driven for a while, that had flat tires, that were cobwebbed. Maybe 10 people would call back, he'd talk to them about what was wrong with the cars, and he might buy one or two for $100 or $150, ones that didn't need serious work. He'd wash them, get them back running again, and sell them for twice as much as he'd bought them for. He always had several cars he was working on around the house.

So, in his room, I went through some of the ways I approached shoplifting, and he was intrigued. So intrigued, that my mom got a call from his mom, perhaps a week later, telling my mom that I'd taught Tom how to steal briefcases from stores. That was because Tom had stolen one, and hadn't hid it all that well from a mom who was a bit more suspicious of her son's activities than my mom.

I can't remember if he had to return the briefcase or not, but that created a minor storm for a bit with my mom, and was one of the few times in those early days I was associated with theft in my parents' house, though my mom likely remembered the candy incident from my sugar-head youth. I was also pretty pissed that Tom had implicated me to his mother, particularly because I knew him to be a fairly skillful liar at that point.

But it all blew over. I didn't ever steal a briefcase again, but then again, they never went with my outfits. But I didn't need to steal briefcases to keep in practice. I was just beginning to hit my stride.

CHAPTER SEVEN

The Criminal Master—Well, Mini-Mind

Being a 16-year-old boy, it wasn't all about the shop-lifting. I looked longingly at the girls in high school, but I was never much of a player. I could make some of them laugh, but not in close quarters. At least, not close enough for me. But I managed to get an actual girlfriend, even if it was only for a few months, and she didn't even go to my high school. That's because she was still 14.

I met Pam at my new hangout house, the McKims, where things were always lively. That's because there were a whole lot of McKims. Mark, Michelle and Melani were all close to my age, and friends with neighbor Pam, who was friendly and pretty and sociable. There were younger and older McKims too, saving up for a shortage. I didn't pay a good deal of attention to the additional McKims because they were either too young or too old, and I couldn't be an influencer in their sphere.

Pam and I used to make out in her room, with the door open, so we were pretty cautious, because her father, a burly beast of a guy with a big pompadour who drove a giant polished Toronado, would have liked nothing better than to put me in the big blender he used for his margaritas. Her parents wouldn't let her come to my place, so we hung out at the

McKims a good deal too, when we weren't in Pam's room, me as frustrated at my inept clothes-on groping as I was by the fact that Pam loved Grand Funk Railroad and played their "Closer to Home" album over and over. And over and over.

I never got closer to home with Pam than our extended slobber sessions, and she cooled to me over time, but still remained friendly, though I was steamed that she later had a steamy shower session with the older brother of one of my other high school friends. The McKim household was notable for good parties and good pals, and for my friend Marty having an affair with Michelle's mom that lasted longer than my Funked-up epoch with Pam.

The household was also notable for being next door to Lynn's house. Lynn was the former girlfriend of Denny, as mentioned, one of my oldest friends. She was not a virgin. Decidedly not. Despite my sweaty efforts, I still was. That would change, but later.

About this time, Abbie Hoffman's *Steal This Book* came out. Not only was I impelled to steal the book, but I felt it mandatory to do so. So I did. The book's "Up the establishment" creed offered significant sections on how to get things "free," including information on the virtues and methods of shoplifting.

You see, Hoffman had finally given me the language to justify my shaky moral positioning on theft. I was *sticking it to the man,* though in my middle-class white-kid upbringing, I didn't have a strong clue just who the man might be. With my suburban, vanilla roots, I was as unlikely to be an anarchist as I was an astronaut.

The odd thing—or maybe it wasn't that odd because I was a numbskull teenager and it was a peak of the "fuck the system" days—was that I fundamentally felt no moral compunction about stealing at all. From stores, at least. I felt swell-headedly justified, because I could mouth the words "capitalist pigs," like Abbie, however hazily I understood how the system actually worked. And, as mentioned, my parents would have been mortified, since the fact they wouldn't have stolen a postage stamp from an earl only tickled my dormant conscience on rare occasions. I still don't know why my blood-infused Catholic guilt didn't kick in with any kick until long in the shoplifting future.

I'm pleased that I didn't take any of Abbie's advice on how to make homemade bombs, but taking corporate goods— oh yeah. I had a splendidly gaseous way of haughtily declaring that the man was being stuck to by my "liberating" these products.

At this point, I was stealing things for fun as much as for the money. I'd expanded my range of operations some: I stole Hoffman's book from a bookstore at the multi-boulevard complex of stores not far from my high school. Across a big intersection, they included a movie theater, big grocery stores, drug stores, bowling alley, and a host of restaurants and small shops. Not far from the bookstore was a tobacconist, where I was spending some of my shoplifting cash on cigars.

I'd graduated from the criminal baseness of those early Tiparillos to real cigars, and real cigars, like a Joya de Nicaragua or Macanudo or La Gloria de Cubana cost several dollars. A pittance of what they cost today, but still pricey for a high school kid. There was an interim period where I smoked the packaged cigars that were a step up from the Tiparillos or Swisher Sweets, like Antonio y Cleopatra and Garcia y Vega. But still, these were machine-made cigars, made with scrap, short-filler tobacco.

The advantage for me of those mid-range stogies, other than not causing a premature death like the Tiparillos surely would have, was that they were also sold in convenient 5-packs, and sold in regular—that is, not closely observed—stores, not in the close-quarter tobacconists' shops with walk-in humidors. In other words, those small boxes of cigars were easy to steal.

I did pocket those for a while, but I tired of the narrow flavors of those commercial-grade stogies. Once I tried a premium, hand-rolled cigar from Honduras, or the Dominican Republic or Nicaragua, I didn't go back to the 5-packs, despite the price—free—being right.

I did manage to lift some of the premium cigars from a couple of shops in the area, but the proprietors were so nice and personable that I felt some guilt, and stopped. (See, I *could* feel guilt, but that was only a hobby, not a vocation.)

So, I'd begun smoking hand-rolled stogies, though still not at home, though I'm sure my parents must have smelled tobacco on me now and then. My taste in booze was changing too: I still drank some Scotch when I could manage to pilfer it, but after getting a snootful of American whiskey, like Jack Daniel's and Wild Turkey, my senses aligned more in that direction. Brown liquor good.

That was reinforced by an evening when I'd invited some of my friends over to spend the night in my parents' garage, and everyone enthusiastically downed my servings of Grape Crush and vodka. Until those servings started coming colorfully back up, all over the garage floor. I couldn't drink vodka again for years.

I was getting a little too big for my britches (or my thefts were getting too big for them) when the incident I described in the introduction happened with the 8-track player in the Two Guys store. That was sometime during the summer, between my sophomore and junior years in high school, the moment where the plainclothes cop in Two Guys tapped me on the shoulder and I ditched the goods and took off.

At that point, it had been a while since I'd been caught, so maybe my vigilance was slipping. My good sense definitely was: a home 8-track player—and this was a fancy one, framed in a heavy wood case with large chrome dials—was a substantial thing, much bigger and heavier than a cassette deck. I'd used what had become a tried-and-true method there, with the store-labeled bag and the stapled receipt, but the detective must have spotted the wild-haired idiot stuffing this heavy object in a big bag in the electronics aisle, and he knew he had a live one.

So, I did get away, but it would be a while, as was the case for The Broadway, that I'd step in that store again. That experience with the tape player chastened me. I became more cautious, more watchful. Even though when I went into a store at that time, any store, and immediately size it up for shoplifting potential, I wouldn't take anything at first unless it was a sure thing.

I scouted paths I would run if I were caught, ways to circle back home. I very much checked out other people in the store, much more so than before, and was warier than ever of the "eye in the sky" boxes, and where their store views were clear and where they were not. I also practiced, like a theater student, nonchalant or deadpan looks in the mirror.

But I never practiced not stealing.

Most people associate the first gas crisis with OPEC proclaiming an oil embargo in 1973. That did indeed rocket gas prices in a number of countries, the U.S. included. But there was an earlier gas crisis that didn't get much publicity. That's because it was a crisis for a number of my high school classmates in the fall of 1971.

The crisis was that a number of my pals had cars (though I wasn't among them), and that we wanted to go places in them, but no one had much money. Stealing gas from gas stations was impractical. Stealing gas from random cars was chancy, and if you got a swallow of gas from the hose you stuck in someone's tank while you were trying to siphon two-thirds of a gallon from some innocent, you'd remember it for hours, because a gasoline burp is one of life's miseries. (I speak from experience.)

Also, stealing gas from a random car didn't simply go into a random gray area of ethics. The shade was decidedly darker. It was challenging to say that you were "sticking it to the man," if by the man you couldn't point to a corporate entity that owned 100 department stores, but instead you were sticking it to some guy named Ralph, who was perhaps a grocery store clerk whose car, parked six blocks over from your suburban neighborhood, was left unguarded one early evening. You didn't really want to think that you were sticking it to Ralph. So I tried not to think about it.

We didn't bring up the Ralphs or the Mabels or all the other innocent drivers all that often when we went on a gas-stealing binge for a month or three, all courtesy of Tom's invention. I mentioned Tom earlier, the briefcase master, no? I also mentioned that he was quite the mechanic. He outdid himself with his gas-thieving mechanism. Tom used to hang out at the Long Beach Yacht Club (I think he knew somebody there, and he was interested in sailing) and he somehow managed to get his hands on an old manual bilge pump for a boat.

This basically looked like one of those old hand-cranked water pumps you might see in the "Beverly Hillbillies," which they showed Jethro working in the old days: it was an upright cylinder, several feet tall, with a long metal handle, and input and outflow hoses.

Tom had the bright idea to mount it on the floor in the middle of the back of a Volkswagen bus, of which he had a couple. We could pull next to a car in a parking lot, open one of the swinging back doors of his bus, open the gas cap of the car opposite, slip the hose in, and pump five gallons of gas in a couple of minutes. The bilge pump was that powerful, and the operation was swift, and he had the 5-gallon gas cans. If it was an evening going to darkness, a person could walk by and not notice anything happening, unless they looked closely.

But no one ever looked.

OK, that was a crummy thing to do. That wasn't stealing records from Sav-On, though it's arguable that those thievings as well were all of a piece in regards to ethics, and that piece was cracked. But I wasn't thinking that way when I was turning 17. I was still thinking, "Wow, I can steal stuff. And not get caught." Well, rarely get caught. The moral ambiguity became worse later, as you'll see. But before we go into how we struck out at all the available innocent Ralphs in the world in a more devious way, I'll take a detour into absolute shame.

One of the things we did as a group (some combination of my brother, Marty, Denny, Ron, possibly Tom, me, maybe Matt; Zack was innocent, only because he was still in Canada) was jolly: we would fill a refillable fire extinguisher—some of them had screw-off caps, and could be pressurized with a gas-station air hose—with water. And sometimes water and other things, which included vinegar, Kool-Aid, and urine. Yes, we'd pee in the canister.

Then we'd pressurize it and look for people to bother. And by bother, I mean spray. We'd drive around and stop where a person was on a corner and say, "Hey, do you know where the [insert fake store/building/house name here"] is?" And then we'd spray them out the window with the extinguisher and drive away. We found that hilarious. I warned you earlier about teenage boys.

Again, we did that for a temporary period, maybe the months we did stealing the gas. We had people run after us, cursing. We sprayed a guy on a 10-speed once and had to stop for a traffic signal and he caught up with us, screaming curses. So, we were morons. But that pales to something I did sometime in that period, the thing that is in the top three of Most Shameful Things I've Done. We were driving around, having stopped at a favorite fast-food place to get burgers and fries and malts.

This particular place, long before the Big Gulp, sold GIANT malts for a dollar, probably a quart or so. I could normally take that right down, because, sugar. But on this summer day, driving with the windows down, I had about a third of it left. I was in the back seat, curbside and we were slowing to turn at a traffic-signal intersection and I saw a guy standing close to the curb and cleverly thought I could just toss the rest of my malt on him.

Which I did. I only got a glimpse of the guy after we'd rounded the corner and were speeding away. He was a small man, neatly dressed in a suit. That is, neatly dressed before I'd hit him with the malt, which covered the front of his clothes. He was Asian, middle-aged. I looked back at that guy and felt instant shame. I feel shame while I'm typing this. Maybe that guy was going to a church service, a funeral, a wedding, and he gets assaulted for no reason.

I wondered forever if he thought it was a racist act, but I hadn't known he was Asian until after I'd trashed him. It was a stupid, callous act for sure. After I did it, I laughed a little, uncomfortably and someone said something like "Shit, you really got that guy!" but there wasn't much enthusiasm.

I'm not sure why we stopped stealing gas or spraying people. Maybe we were tired of smelling like gasoline when we'd slosh it on ourselves, maybe the friends with cars got a quarter raise at the pizza parlor and felt more flush—who knows? Maybe having angry people yell at us got old. Or maybe me throwing a malt for no good fucked-up reason at some random person slowly broke down our sense of "let's go fuck with people." But those particular dark deeds stopped not all that long after they started. However, there were some replacements.

CHAPTER EIGHT

Senior Discounts

My own shoplifting work continued apace. Records and cassettes and tape decks, yes. The occasional larger piece of electronics? Yes, though never again something as bulky—at least as a "walk out of the store like you owned it" item—as that home 8-track I'd been caught with.

I also did goofy thefts, that were again morally negligent, at various points in my career. Going way back, I invented, if you want to call it something as gaudy as an invention, a "low-price bulb snatcher," which was a cardboard toilet-paper roll taped to the end of a broomstick. To what end did I employ this noble device? To steal Christmas bulbs from houses on the periphery of our neighborhood. In those early adolescent days, Matt, Zack and I did this, with some zest.

With my outstanding science skills, I discovered that a toilet-paper roll could be used to grasp, unscrew and hold the standard-size Christmas lights from below, meaning, when they were up on someone's house, illuminating Christmas cheer. What did we do with those Christmas lights, after we'd snatch eight or nine from a house, and then go to the next house? Well, we usually threw them on the street somewhere to hear them pop. Again, science.

So, that was definitely uncool. I think we did that for a couple of Christmases. It might have taken the time that someone caught us, and as we were running away the lights I'd stuffed in my front pockets started breaking, that we stopped, though I'm not sure about that. Maybe Santa threatened us; I just can't remember.

I *can* remember that between my junior and my senior year in high school, I lost my virginity, which was a loss I greatly welcomed. The coordinator of this loss was Lynn, the former girlfriend of Denny, my old pal and neighbor, who took this agreeably, since he and Lynn were broken up by then, and because Dennis was a philosophical sort. Lynn lived next door to the McKims, the menagerie of M's mentioned earlier, so proximity was convenient for all kinds of debauchery. I found sex to be a harmonious celebration, so we celebrated whenever we could. We were all friendly people back then.

Though Lynn and I were together—through acrimonious hurricanes and the mentioned harmonies—for a couple of years, she wasn't a large part of my thieving. However, she helped me remain dicey with the law by encouraging me to take her father's motorcycle out of his garage while he was at work one day, and we drove down to Laguna Beach.

That was all fine, except when the cop pulled us over because, as Lynn explained, "I was pretending to push the motorcycle along with the bottoms of my feet." So, the cop who saw this girl winging her legs back and forth freely on the back of the bike thought it had no passenger foot pedals, which it did. However, he only found that out after finding out that I didn't have a motorcycle license, and he gave me a ticket.

A copy of the citation arrived in Lynn's father's mail a few days after that. He told her to tell me if he ever saw me at his house, he'd put a bullet in my head. At least he didn't tell it to my face, like the father of my friend Ron, who went apoplectic after Ron's stepmom realized that someone had slept on her bed in her room while they were out of town.

That someone was me, and the cooperating someone was Lynn. The uncooperating love remnants were on Ron's step-mother's lavender bedspread. (Which matched, without exaggeration, everything in the room. She had cornered the world's lavender-colored market.)

The next time I was at Ron's house, his father, a very tall, angry-most-of-the-time man, shouted, two inches from my face, "You frizzy-haired bastard! Don't ever come over here again!" From that point, Ron was told never to have any of his friends over to his house. So we never did go over. Except when his parents weren't home.

But I was careful not to move any of the approximately one thousand bottles of perfume in their bedroom—all in lavender-colored bottles—even half an inch, because Ron's stepmom knew the to-the-millimeter location of every bottle. I never left stains on the lavender bedspread again either, courteous boy me. Fathers of daughters would continue to admire me for years to come.

I must claim one more victory against the faceless bureaucrats who tormented me: yes, those high school public-servant torturers. Since we were still in the Dark Ages when I attended high school, it was still necessary to bring a note from your mom or dad or doctor if you missed class. You'd bring that to the desk at the main office, they'd try to determine if it was a clear forgery or good enough to not argue about it, and they'd give you a date-stamped "re-admit" slip, which you'd show to your teachers, so they could mark you as an excused absence on their rosters.

Now I had indeed forged a note or two in my time. But my handwriting is a thing of Dante's Inferno and it was hard to get my demon scrawl to cooperate. So I did the next best— really, even better—thing: I snagged a blank pad of re-admit sheets from an unoccupied desk in the school office. The way the things work is that they'd hand-write your name, date of absence and other info on the sheet, and then run it under an electric date-stamp machine that printed the date and time of day on the paper, in red ink.

I'd noticed before that the printed date-stamp looked a lot like the output from one of those hand-held date stampers, the kind that have a rotating-wheel cylinder where you spin the numbers into alignment. Here's the real miracle: I PAID (what came over me?) for one of those little stampers in an office store, and indeed, when I compared the results from a real office re-admit to my efforts with stamping the dates, they were nearly identical. Close enough so that any harried teacher, who would just glance at you, the sheet and the date-stamp and mark it in their books, would buy it.

They did. I used those re-admits for me when I played hooky, and for some friends of mine as well. I felt there were many more diverting educational opportunities out of the classroom, and had to pursue them. But spending a full day out of school was an infrequent pleasure—sometimes we'd just use the re-admits for missing a class or two.

One other high-school diversion that my friends and I gleefully participated in was as anti-high school propagandists, but in the most charming of ways, of course. That charm originated from a wholly innocent acquisition of mine, a thing I found in an old desk drawer. Whose old desk drawer is lost in the pages of time. That find was a three-inch or so metal stamp with a handle that when inked could impress a small image on paper, with fair detail, of a man's face, with his name, Frank W. Lloyd printed below.

From Frank's hairstyle and suit, he appeared to be a friendly fellow from 1940 or so, perhaps a real-estate agent or country-fair magician or pomaded con man who liked to stamp his documents, or his letters or his children with his own image and name.

We didn't know Frank's history, so we gave him one. He became the face, spokesperson and jolly nemesis of the Millikan High's administrators (and some teachers). How did our flat-faced Frank do this? Because we channeled Frank's inner loathing of dull high school practices, by producing a series (and a series that lasted at least a year) of posters and proclamations suggesting that Frank had the inside scoop on school scandals (which we made up), personal proclivities of disliked teachers and administrators and of narcs, and general observations about society and the injustices of the Vietnam War.

The posters might say something as riotously clever as "Frank W. Lloyd says don't smoke while doing your homework," with a cut-out, pasted-on image of Godzilla breathing fire, and the ubiquitous Lloyd stamp at the bottom of every one. There were many variations of the old Burma Shave signs: "A chicken in every pot. Or pot in every chicken, as Frank W. Lloyd says."

We particularly delighted in tormenting the snowy-haired principal, Clarence Wood, by either pasting on images of a man doing ridiculous things or drawing an image, and attributing the lunatic acts to our principal, reported by Frank W. Lloyd. That his first name was Clarence and his last Wood fueled many—adolescent—turns of phrase.

We'd sometimes make multiple copies of the posters and then tape them up in school hallways when no one was looking. Mr. Lloyd ran for student-body president and other prestigious offices, as well as wrote poetry, mused on the tastes of the time, and made fun of school traditions. Marty, Dennis, Tom and I were deeply involved in the production and the postering. Dennis got caught throwing a bunch of little leaflets with Frank's firm face on them over a balcony at a school event, and was reprimanded.

At a later point, after administrative exasperation had set in, Marty got caught putting up a poster, and was suspended from school, and his parents protested, citing the First Amendment. And Marty didn't rat the rest of us out, but that event tempered our postering persistence.

High school was a boring obligation to many of us, and we often had to create our own amusements. Millikan High pep rallies were not among them, but making fun of them was. Well, *we* thought it was funny, but individual tastes do vary.

By this point, I'd had some mild involvement with the police on a few occasions: I was handcuffed and taken down to a Long Beach station (and quickly released) after throwing firecrackers at a football game. I was ticketed for hitchhiking on the freeway with Lynn once where my carefully crafted alias, with false name and address that I'd made her memorize (after I'd long had it memorized should the occasion arise) was discovered to be immediately false, because I told the cops my fake name and she told them my real name.

That pissed off the one cop who was questioning me so much that he turned me face-forward on the side of his cruiser, cuffed me and literally—this is not something I would make up—drew his gun and put it slightly between my legs while he yelled at me asking me for my real name.

Now I probably did look like a terrorist, or perhaps a homeless person, but that alarmed me a good deal. But the cops finally let us go after giving us a ticket and a warning. That ticket, which went unpaid, turned into problem months later when cops pulled us all over in Marty's van (running joke of that time: VW van sighting = probable cause), and at that point I was carrying a driver's license and they ran it and found I had a warrant for that unpaid ticket. I was taken to a downtown station for that too, and I don't remember who bailed me out, though it wasn't my parents. Bail and its lack will play a significant part in my later tale of deeper involvement with the justice system.

Senior-year shoplifting remained pretty consistent: I was still using the store-label bags and stapler for records and sometimes clothes, still taking orders from my friends for various things, still stealing liquor (half-pints of Wild Turkey began to frequently make their now-you-see-it, now-you-don't into my coat), mostly wine and whiskey, but more whiskey, because half-pints were easy and wine bottles were not.

One of the lovely ironies of my senior year was that for a period of months, I was a Jesus Freak, as we dubbed ourselves back then. What led me to Jesus? Sex, of course. One of the more prominent born-agains was this lovely senior girl named Ann, who sometimes led visible gatherings of fresh-faced New Testament-toters outside on school lawns at lunchtime. I thought she was a striking one, so I listened on the periphery a bit. Having spent so much time in Catholic school, the teachings of the Bible seemed old hat to me, and since I was by then heartily engaged in both shoplifting and drug taking, nothing there was going to stick.

Until I saw Ann's sister, Joyce. I thought Ann was striking, but Joyce, a sophomore, blindsided me. Beautiful, athletic, very long shimmering blond hair, a big, open smile. I was dumbstruck. So dumbstruck that even though Lynn and I were still dating, I figured out Joyce's schedule, so that I would stand on a bench in the areas where she would walk by between classes and stare at her. She had the good sense to ignore my stalking, so I started going to the Bible studies, where at first I merely sat behind her and tried to send telepathic messages of my devotion.

But she was impervious to my passion, so I had to actually talk to her. We became friends, and I was more thunderstruck by her warm, open and modest personality—she seemed to honestly not know how lovely and smart she was. That began a period of several-days-and-nights-a-week gatherings of Jesus Freaks, from Bible studies at someone's house to small groups in small evangelical churches (with laying on of hands and speaking in tongues, which is good if you want to practice your alien languages) to vast assemblages of people—in the thousands—in giant Southern California Christian churches.

I dialed back my shoplifting for a while, and my pot intake as well. So did Matt, who remained a Jesus Freak for a longer period than me (and had a Christian girlfriend as well). But when Joyce and I started seeing each other outside of those gatherings, and I began to see a lot of examples of one-upmanship, political maneuvering and treachery in Millikan's Christian groups, I resumed my sinful ways. Not as her boyfriend for a long while, but as her lustful-though-trying-to-hide-it friend.

Much to Joyce's father's chagrin, since I was deep in my barefoot phase (and was as hairy as most primates), Joyce and I started visiting each other semi-regularly; her house was only a few blocks from mine. She was a splendid Frisbee player: she could toss a Frisbee a dazzling distance and loved to romp a distance to catch one, and we played often in the sun in a nearby park.

In the next year and a half, I broke up with Lynn perhaps 10 times, partially inspired by my interest in Joyce and partially because of differences in temperament between me and Lynn. There were many vehement exchanges on both sides in that volatile breakup zone, and emotional casualty, but no blood. You will hear of Joyce's sad fate later.

Sometime during that last school year, I stole, from my Millikan high school library, a book titled *Willie Mays: My Secrets of Playing Baseball.* There is another one of those ethical contradictions: I loved libraries, thought they were houses of worship almost, and had spent so many absorbed hours in them as a kid. But here I stole that book, a book about one of my heroes. And I still have that book.

If my mom knew, she might march me back to my high school to return the book, but she's in heaven, and would probably just laugh anyway. I don't have any justification for stealing from libraries, places I cherished, other than that humans, strange creatures that they are, can rationalize some of the most godawful things. It's clear the devil made me do it.

I had become enamored of the Grateful Dead between '71 and '72, through the persuasions of Big Joe, a school friend who was in a Dead cover band and who later became my old neighborhood pal Janet's husband. One of the band's buddies was Marc, who among his other skills, peddled some fine acid at school. At one point, I may have traded some stolen Dead records for acid, but one memory of mine is certain: Marc had me hold a small container of blotter acid at high school for him for several hours, when he thought the "narcs" were going to search him. We called the security officers the narcs, because searching for stoned kids and their stoner goods was part of their job.

I was truly honored that Marc had asked me to hold the acid, because I only knew him peripherally, and I was desperate for anyone to think I was cool. We met much later in the day and he took his acid back. But I knew who to turn to when I wanted to buy some acid for my first Dead concert, which was scheduled for the Hollywood Bowl on June 17, 1972—a Sunday. A big day, because I'd graduated from high school two days before.

A big night, because all of us—Matt, Denny, Ron, Lynn, me—were very high, because the windowpane that Marc had sold us was very good. It was a beautiful early summer's eve, it was the delightful outdoor setting of the Hollywood Bowl, and it was the Dead, a band I'd grown to love through the recordings, but as everyone knew, it was playing live where they shone.

And it was the end of high school.

That meant a lot to me, because I'd long felt stifled at school, geeky and out of place. I'd made good friends, but never felt at ease or engaged, or very interested in the academics. I'd done fine on paper in my classes, though my math understandings were pathetic. I never quite meshed with the "in" groups. Not athletic enough (though I tried) to be an athlete, not stoned enough (though I tried) to be a stoner, not social enough to be a "sosh," not menacing enough to be a low-rider, not blond enough to be a surfer.

The shades of being an outsider—alienation, resentment, jealousy, pride—and in the extremes, mental illness, can make a character behave in devious ways. Devious was something I was good at.

Back to the concert: it was fabulous. We were back from the main stage a fair distance, a couple of tiers from the floor level. The Dead played some of their classics, they wound up the crowd, pulled them in, pushed them away, pulled them back at higher volume. Except for my brother, who didn't drop acid (since he was driving, thank the stars), we were all soaring, particularly Denny, who was swaying so much to the music I thought he was sure to fall over the small wall he was standing on, dividing us from a lower level.

One of the great contrasts in that concert was that I was in ecstasy over the music, yet rabid over some security goons who punched a couple of people from our level who'd jumped over the wall to get closer to the scene. The goons were apparently college football players who'd been hired for security and they popped a few people pretty good directly below us, and those confrontations happened a few times. So, when we weren't flying to the music, we were yelling at the security to back off.

Those guys had armbands that said "Peace Power," but peaceful it wasn't. The concert marked the last performance of

Pigpen, the Dead's keyboardist before his early death. He didn't sing at all, and just played some listless notes, never going into the big blues persona he carried so well. Thus began the curse of prematurely dead Dead keyboard players over the succeeding years.

We lived though, and returned to Matt's house, where his parents were gone for the night. We had bought an entire case of Reese's Peanut Butter Cups, eternally one of my favorite candies. They were even more stimulating while coming down from acid, which can take 10–14 hours, but can feel like a few weeks. I remember being entranced by Ron swimming underwater laps naked in Matt's pool in its soft blue lights. Ron was about six-four and weighed perhaps 140 pounds, and watching him scissor through the water with those long, long legs did make you wonder if he was an extraterrestrial. Or perhaps that was just me.

Ron was living at my house at that point, because his tough-guy dad had kicked him out, maybe because Ron forgot to say "sir" when he asked him a question. Look up "uptight" in the dictionary, and you'll see Ron's father's photo. Anyway, my mother and father both liked Ron, and my drafted brother Rick was soon to go in the Army, so there was room. My parents were always generous, always friendly to my friends, even though my dad called Denny "Charlie Manson" because of his hair and beard. My hair and beard would soon be on the march as well.

So, I'd made it through high school, which seemed miracle enough. More so that I wasn't in jail, but not for lack of trying. I was a study in contradictions, in that I loved reading and writing, but loathed the formal school setting. But perhaps that's not surprising, because taking a pocket, shallow analysis of our learning institutions told anyone that conformity and uniformity was encouraged in most school structures.

Good academic performance, of the straight and narrow kind, was encouraged and rewarded. Eccentricity or weirdo leanings weren't exactly suppressed (unless you were perhaps something other than a middle-class white kid), but were treated with a "he'll get over it" roll of the eyes.

I definitely had the weirdo leanings. I was fascinated by the worlds far from my suburban life. I earlier mentioned Phil, my sister's friend, who had first turned me on to pot. My oldest sister Colleen's friend, Phil was years older than my crowd, but he liked to hang out with us once in a while. He was gay, and definitely not in the closet. He was a striking looking guy, Italian, not particularly tall, but handsome and personable.

He loved the gay party scene in Hollywood, and more than once took a bunch of us to hang out in gay bars in and around Hollywood. I met my first drag queens (in a Hollywood Denny's, of all places), and leather boys, and perhaps a trans person or two, but I didn't have a clue about that back then. I remember going to a nightclub where Phil had to do some coded knock on the door and a guy slid back a metal plate covering a slit to inspect us and decide whether to let us in. He did.

Me being 16 and in later jaunts, 17, and my friends and my brother near the same ages, us being allowed in gay bars was a strange, exciting treat. Of course, we were still teenage straight boys who sometimes called each other "fags" and "homos," so we weren't progressive on those counts (few counts, really), but Phil was our friend, and made for great company. It took a while for any actual social consciousness on gay rights issues to kick in.

One time in Long Beach a group of us went into a fancy, crowded hotel lobby and were walking toward a restaurant when Phil fainted and fell to the floor. Several employees rushed up and tried to rouse him and he struggled to his feet. Later he just laughed in his maniacal high-pitched way, saying he loved to cause a commotion. He called other men "bitches" long before it became a common term, and called us "girl" when he wanted to make a point: "Oh girl, you know better than that!" He was charming, and slightly dangerous, and I liked that.

I didn't like that I continued to have mildly depressive episodes, a component of the anxiety I mentioned earlier, where the world felt gray to me, or muffled, like a shirt pulled over my head. I'd had those periods, which could last a week or more, since I was 15. I was probably doing a poorly intellectualized version of nihilism as I then understood it, likely because I'd seen the word in a book I'd read. I'd had a brief Sartre/Camus period, one where I probably left the books in a conspicuous place so people could see I was reading them.

I likely talked myself into thinking I was depressed, because it seemed to be associated with artists and creativity, and had a cachet. I wish it was as easy to talk myself out of being depressed, because those claws have hung on for all these years. (Oh, if you ever get to thinking depression is cool—it's not.)

I mixed that ersatz allure of gloom with readings from Zen Buddhist texts, where you can take various flavors of "the external world is meaningless" and that we as societies were merely going through the motions, and shape that into a "nothing matters" mantra. So I constructed a little dime-store philosophy to go along with my shoplifting. I was way ahead of my time: I could have started online courses in a kind of anarchic liberation theology, if there only was an online at the time.

But who needs online when you can hit the road?

On the Road, Eyes (and Pockets) Wide Open

Sometime in that early summer of high school liberation, I met Zack at his parents' house in Vancouver,
and we decided to hitchhike east, as far as we could go and
then come back. In reflecting on it now, it surprises me his
parents let him go. His mom, Aida, is a wonderful woman but a
perennial worrier, and his dad, though with some mad streaks
himself, could be persuaded by her. But not this time.

We were on the road for a month or so, making it to a
small town in central Ontario—and then back, which seems a
minor miracle of survival. A few highlights: Drivers driving
stolen cars, drivers who tell you that they are JUST coming on
to their first hits of acid (and smiling at you in that special way
as they accelerate to lunatic speed); a driver—in a business
suit, no less—pulling out a gun, "just to show you that there
won't be any problems"; a van full of people ALL on acid, playing Blue Oyster Cult at ear-bleeding volume, and insisting, and
I mean *insisting,* that you ride with them for HOURS; drivers
who wept, cursed and wanted so much to share their tiny
chewed rag of worldly experience that they could so succinct-
ly express ... in 17 chapters, blow-by-blow as you weakly nod.

Best of all were the Suckahead Brothers (so dubbed because every sentence began with the epithet "Suckahead! Did

you see that chick in the Pontiac!"), who were driving what had to be a stolen truck for almost the entire distance of our return trip, picking up people left and right because they had no money at all (or professed such), cadging it from the riders for gas and food. We rode over 1,000 miles with them back west to Vancouver, grouped with an ever-replenished truck-bed of fellow hitchhikers, never less than 10 at a time, often 15 or more, so that people periodically would stand up screeching "Cramp! Cramp!" because there was no place to stretch your legs.

The brothers would NOT stop for anything except their own needs; one of their favorite tricks was to get a desperate rider (*desperate* being my middle name) to have to pee out the side of the truck, and then to vary their lurching speeds so that it was like peeing in a fan back at you. Oh, they did make an exception to stop when they picked up a waitress from a cafe and on the spot convinced her to ride with us (still in her uniform), so she rode up front, and because one of them was desperate to win her favor, let her drive a manual-tranny truck outside of Banff on the Trans-Canada Highway at high speed with 16 people in the truck. She'd never driven a stick before.

And they were urging her to pass cars on the whippy blind-corner roads at speed, which she did. They did stop for a couple of hours to let the enamored brother have sex with her in the cab of the truck while we waited. However, they were polite enough to warn us: another couple, two absolute strangers who had been picked up separately, had sex IN the truck while the Suckaheads drove. There were at least 10 other people riding along (though most were sleeping; I wasn't). The coupling couple had only known each other for a couple of hours.

I was able to refine some of my shoplifting techniques on that trip, because we were starving and had less than five bucks between us for the return, so Zack and I would go into grocery stores, buy a tiny package of cheese and crackers, while we stuffed the backpacks we wore with things like cooked chickens from those heated standalone barbecue areas some big markets have. Plus zillions of candy bars.

That journey was one of those condensed periods during which I was exposed to people the likes of which I'd never met; I could tell a thousand stories from that trip (and I did—I wrote a bad novel based on that experience).

One consequence of riding in the back of a pickup for several days straight was that when I got back to Vancouver, when I released my hair (which at that time was a combination of Jimi Hendrix by way of Albert Einstein, but longer), it stayed in its beaver-tail-like ponytail. It had become a thing unto itself on the road, a wide, flat integrated object, not a mane of individual hairs. Zack's mom had to chop the whole thing off, because no conditioner could untangle it. I'm sure the Department of Defense could have used it for weapons research.

Another event not long after that Canadian odyssey took me by a quite roundabout method to a whorehouse in Juarez, Mexico in the later summer of '72, though that destination wasn't in the plans. That's because the plans were very loose. Most 17-year-olds aren't known for their careful planning, and I was no exception. So when my friend Marty offered me one of two 30-day Greyhound tickets he'd been given, I jumped at the free travel opportunity. The complication was that the tickets only had three days' value left on them, but that simply focused our goal: go as far as possible and then turn around and come back. Three days' journey on an outbound Dog might not seem like a rich travel experience, but I'd lived in LA County for all my life, that good Catholic boy, and right then, a bus moving anywhere sounded like a good thing.

A Greyhound agent told us, a bit off the record, that the passes had a contingency where if you were heading back to your destination when they expired, they would honor the journey to its end. That put a little more highway onto our hopes, and after debating directions and destinations, we settled on the edge of Texas. El Paso, to be exact, arriving from Long Beach in about two and a half days, where we intended do an about-bus, and trek back from whence we came. We didn't know a thing about El Paso, just that it now signified the boundary in the distance, the edge of our map.

To begin, we pushed through the bleak sunburnt soul of southern California on Highway 40, heading east, absorbing all the staccato beats of the bus: the engine's steady droning through bland landscapes, the glaze-eyed hypnosis broken by sudden passages into small and mid-sized towns, usually approached through the industrial districts. There was a blurry

10-minute stop here and a brisk-walk-down-Main Street forty-minute stop there, and then back in the bus, sprawled in our little leatherette boxes.

Through it all, we just tried to roll with the rhythms of the road, and roll we did, through Arizona and New Mexico, where in Albuquerque, we took a highway hook, stopping the eastward drift and dropping down south. That finally plunked us smack dab into El Paso, where we were going to turn around and reverse our outbound orbit.

But as it happened, El Paso was the longest stopover—five hours—of all of our highway hijinks, and even though we came into town after 10pm, it was Saturday night. Plus, there was an exotic element to our El Paso escapade. Right on the other side of the Rio Grande, Mexico had given one of its classic border towns to the world: Juarez, a foreign country, just a couple of short blocks from the Greyhound station! (This was long before the cartels made fun jaunts in Juarez a bit less fun.)

We walked the bridge and passed through the turnstiles, which to our great amusement, required three cents for the passage. We had no idea of what we wanted to do in Juarez, but our answer appeared behind us in the form of Tony, a young Mexican guy with a green card. Tony was just getting off work in El Paso and heading for a night out in Juarez. His English was good and his attitude better, and he offered to show us some lively spots in the city.

We readily accepted, and we were soon in a big crowded bar, where a loud band was singing mangled Beatles songs in a sloppy but happy hybrid of English and Spanish. Tony shepherded us to the bar, where I had my first boilermaker, amazed that the bartenders would drop the whiskey shot, glass and all, down into the mug of beer. One good glass deserves another, and with no ID check to interfere, we met our Texas thirst head-on.

The bar was almost a warehouse, with a raucous atmosphere that had the joint jumping. There seemed to be mini-dramas at every corner, arguments, crazed laughter, disappointment, but I could only gape at it all, trying to read the body language, my high school Spanish useless. After a few drinks, Tony seemed restless, and he was happy when I asked if there was anywhere around to buy a cigar. Having been smoking those occasional cigars for the past couple of years, it seemed to me that a good stogie would cap a night out in Juarez.

But Tony wasn't exactly thinking of cigars. He directed our taxi through the warm, humid night to a series of small, dimly lit old buildings. We followed him into the largest one, and it was unlike any cigar store I'd ever seen. We were in a large room that was almost wholly lit with candles, big and small. The atmosphere was heavy with some rich perfume, with the flickering candles (and the alcohol) steering my eyes unsteadily around the room.

There was a bar in one corner, around which were several big overstuffed chairs. Along the wall was a huge lime-green couch, above which was a large picture of the Virgin Mary. A pair of young girls dressed in shorts and light blouses sat on the couch. One of them rose and greeted Tony with a smile and a high chattering voice.

They had a quick conversation in Spanish, and then headed through a door leading out back. Tony winked and said he'd be back in a short while. At 17, I wasn't wholly unfamiliar with the ways of the flesh, but I wasn't exactly a suave Lothario, and it took a few beats for me to realize that we were in a whorehouse.

It became clearer when another young girl appeared, and she led Marty and me to the brilliant couch. Both girls seemed to act in unison: my escort put her hand on my leg almost simultaneous with the other putting hers on Marty's. And their questions were nearly identical, something like, "Hello, I Maria, you buy me drink?"

I was a little taken aback by everything, but I gumballed out a strangled "Yes," as did Marty. Soon, they came back from the little bar with some watery beer for all of us, which tallied up to around $20.00. We were both so flummoxed to be where we were, in such delicate company, that we each peeled off a ten—which made our collective cash for the return home about two dollars apiece.

And which also made any thought of a two a.m. tryst with any of these sociable sorority sisters a moot point, which I felt was a relief. We all sat on the shocking couch and smiled and mumbled and looked at the shimmering scene. A few minutes later, Tony popped back in, saving us the embarrassment of ordering anything else on the menu—we had no money for liquor or for love, and at that point, I wasn't certain if I wanted either.

Tony provided for the taxi back to the border, and as the TexMex night slipped away, we got on the bus for the long, long ride home.

That ride back was a blur-eyed haze. One of the few things I remember was being in the seat adjacent and across the aisle from the bathroom, and when the bus driver took a hard turn on the road, a heavy girl, whose pants were around her knees, flew out of the bathroom into my seat. Since I was lounging sideways (Marty was doing the same in a seat further up), she essentially fell into my lap. It wasn't love at first sight.

One other lowlight was Marty and I getting caught stealing food in a Salt Lake City supermarket, probably a Safeway near the Greyhound station, and then getting interrogated in a windowless office by the two straightest men in the world, both of indistinguishable age, both with horn-rimmed glasses, white shirts and black pants, both probably able to tell by looking at us that we'd been in a Juarez whorehouse the day before. (Probably not, but that's how it felt.)

They let us go, and we were still able to get on the bus back.

All I took back from the trip was that kind of numbed brain brought about by extended bouts of busing, with strange visions of flaming lime-green couches, and the Virgin Mary laughing through bright-red lipstick. But we made it back without damnation, and not long after I had a good cigar. I yet haven't quite learned how to properly ask for one in Spanish.

I don't know if the Virgin Mary was laughing or crying more about my antics in those days. I still had a religious bent though: one of the wines I used to steal, and one that was a ladder-rung up on the Ripple and T-Bird I pocketed in the past, was Blue Nun. In those days, drinking Blue Nun harkened back a bit to when Zack and I were being classy with our bad cigars and bad wine. But Blue Nun, which as I recall was something sweet like other Liebfraumilchs of its ilk, was thought by other high-school sophisticates to be more of an adult beverage. And I liked playing adult.

Ripple bottles, which were short and stubby, were much easier to steal than a standard 750ml bottle of wine. Something like the long-necked Blue Nun was more difficult: you had to angle the neck of the bottle under your coat across your chest, which could easily flare the coat open or make a distinct bulging crease. Or you could put the bottle upside-down with the bottle's circular base in your armpit, but that was challenging for the weight and shape alone, and because once under your arm, moisture would condense on the cold bottle, making it harder to clamp.

However, I did get away with filching wine from stores without getting caught, and of course Blue Nun put me in mind of my altar-boy days, and when I used to make the nuns blue by trying to get other students to laugh at my jokes in class. One of the other wines that we all agreed was classy to drink (or be seen drinking) was Mateus, the Portuguese rosé that in those days was in a broad, slope-shouldered bottle that would have been a bitch to steal. But I remember drinking some with cronies once, so maybe I stashed it in one of those briefcases I stole. But probably not.

After my brother moved into my sisters' room, I customized it with other classy objects: I had an empty aluminum keg for a chair. I had a ceiling lamp that Tom had helped me build: an old fire extinguisher that he'd attached a light socket to the top of and run the wire through the bottom. The wall opposite the bed had the last passages of Hesse's *Siddhartha* written by Denny in a nice calligraphic hand.

My parents, bless them.

On another wall, opposite each other: a giant poster of Jimi Hendrix in one of his magnificent king-peacock-from-Mars outfits and the other a giant poster of Willie Mays, bat cocked over his shoulder. (I was a lifelong Dodger fan, but I thought that Willie was the best baseball player ever, so I had to live with that contradiction, which in baseball circles, is clearly schizophrenic.)

And just to show you that 1972 was a big, big year, in the early fall, Zack, down for a visit, went with Denny and me on a road trip up north in Denny's '55 Chevy, which was a fun car, though the right-side rear-seat floor panel had been basically melted by the exhaust system, so that you could see the street through it. It would occasionally belch out smoke and a flame, which was not amusing at all for the hitchhiker we picked up who sat above it and told us the car was on fire. We said we knew, and kept driving.

The car also had bald rear tires, and as was usually the case, no one had enough money to pay for new ones and also go on the trip. We found a gas station somewhere north of Santa Barbara that was butted up to a hill above the highway. While Zack was talking to the attendant out front, Denny and I took a couple of correct tires off a rack that was back and off to the side, mostly out of sight, and tossed them down that hill. We then drove back down and put them in the trunk and had them put on at another station.

We didn't get to put that many miles on them though, because karma was itching for payback. We'd heard about the magical Bay Area Rapid Transit (BART) trains that had recently opened, supposedly a technological marvel of speed and sophistication that would transform transportation in the Bay Area. The system was brand new, and we were excited: we decided that we'd stop in the San Leandro station south of Oakland and ride.

Ride we did. We'd smoked a lot of pot beforehand to make the trip comfy, and we rode BART north for a while and then turned around and came back. But when we went out to the parking lot to get back in the car, we couldn't find it.

Now we were indeed stoned, but coming down. We walked all over that lot, which was fairly large, and pretty crowded, but still, we were looking for a '55 Chevy. We argued whether we'd started from the San Leandro lot, we puzzled over which area of the lot we parked in, we groaned. And then we concluded that indeed the car was stolen. Which it was.

Dealing with the cops and the report took a while. We had clothes and sleeping bags and other stuff in the trunk, including a prized leather jacket of Zack's, but at least we had the clothes on our back to hitchhike back home, tails between our legs. They found the car some weeks later, pretty much stripped. The thieves probably noticed that the back floor caught on fire every once in a while, and decided it wasn't worth it.

CHAPTER TEN

Wild and Crazy (and Obnoxious) Guys

That summer seemed like it couldn't end, but as with many of my speculations, I was wrong. I turned 18 back at home, alone, since Rick had gone into the Army. Not having my brother there was a loss, and that was compounded by unease, because the Vietnam War was still raging, and we didn't know if he would have to go overseas.

He had always been generous with me, and gave me money or treated me to something on more than a few occasions (and would do so, foolish lad, with cars and motorcycles and money into the long future). I also had no big brother to play basketball with in the backyard or pitch a tennis ball to in the driveway. And there was no tip jar to steal from now either.

Zack remained up in Vancouver, because he was finishing out his senior year. Then, as time works these things, it became 1973.

I was in my parents' house and restless, but unsure what was next. I was hanging out a bit less with friends, and not pocketing as many goods without paying for them—the two, because of my ego needs, were related. Another influence there was that I was no longer in school, and had fewer people to sell things to, and fewer people to try and impress with my sleight of hand. Though I did have a household friend: Ron had been kicked out of his house by his father, who had made sure for years that Ron understood that he didn't measure up and never would. That's a message that affects a kid for life, and for Ron, it did.

But my parents, who liked Ron (though my father wouldn't have minded if he trimmed his long, long blond hair) invited him to stay with us. My parents, I should mention again, were at ease with young people, and ever generous. The neighborhood kids and other friends would regularly come over, hang out and eat, and that was rarely a problem.

Ron wasn't the pilfering kind, so that also curtailed some of my freewheeling stealing, though I was still doing it, albeit more modestly. Ron was the getting-high kind though. I recall he and I smoking joints a number of times on the grounds of the Mormon church not far from my house, which shows you how liberal I am on the subject of other religions.

There was something significant that happened in that period: I bought a car. My sister Colleen had bought her first new car, a '73 Capri, after owning a bunch of oldies. My father, whom I mentioned worked at Ford for most of his working life, got a significant family discount, so a shiny red Capri brightened up her driveway, which at that point was in a neighborhood mid-way between my parents' house and downtown.

I got her leftovers, a '64 Volkswagen Squareback, which I probably paid her $50 for. That began a long love affair between me and cars, and as with all love affairs, the breakups could be painful. But I was innocent of that back then. At least when it came to automobiles. I've probably owned 40 cars, and many—'62 Caddy, '63 Mercury Monterey, '62 Pontiac Tempest, '71 Volvo P-1800, '81 380SL Benz, '64 Dodge Dart, '74 Celica, '68 Mustang, '65 Studebaker, '65 Ford Galaxie— were sweet vintage rides. But they could be sour on the wallet.

I often alternated buying a Honda or a Toyota after paying for endless repairs to one of those beauties, because then I could drive *by* the mechanics, rather than stopping. But the allure of vintage wheels always pulled me back again.

The VW, like the three or four VWs I would own subsequently, was powered by hamsters who were usually on cigarette breaks. It would have been good if VW had included some kind of winch to help a driver go up hills. And the Squarebacks were odd even for VW: air-cooled, of course, engine in the back, but with weird dual-carbs that didn't increase power but did make the thing more complicated to fix. The motor was affectionately (?) known as the "pancake engine."

And I didn't really have any money to fix it. So I screwed my courage to the sticking place, and did what for years I'd done so much to avoid, and which I'd never recommend to anyone: I got a job. Oh, the humanity!

My pal Denny's stepfather was some kind of exec for the Zody's department store chain, and he got me a job as a salesperson in the audio department at the local Zody's. I even got a haircut, though my hair (and attitude) was still scruffy. We can acknowledge the irony of me working as an audio salesperson in a department store. Many of the relatives of the smaller pieces of audio equipment in the store had made their way into my shopping bags at other stores, no cashier needed.

But it was a while before I'd pull off any Zody's antics like that, and that was as an outside accomplice of Denny's, not as an employee. The Squareback and Zody's had a bit of a reciprocal relationship: I needed a car to get to Zody's and I needed Zody's wages to pay for the car expenses. And probably lots of candy and ice cream. No, some childhood urges never leave.

My boss at Zody's was a good guy, very straight but straightforward too. The other salespeople, of which there were three, were various flavors of weasels, though genial. Two were real backslapping fellows, friends to all, until any potential customers were discovered to be in "just browsing" mode, which is when they would disappear. They also were happy to steal each other's sales, and to describe the customers in withering language, which was also amusing.

The other was a nicer guy, and a better salesperson because of it, but he was also a bit of a conniver. I was fundamentally the servant, dispatched to dust the equipment and take care of customers who asked too many questions without their wallets showing. The salespeople were all older than me by 5–10 years. I was amazed when the nicer one had me take his vehicle to deliver something somewhere one day and I found the inside of his van was a total love den, with purple carpet on the walls and ceiling (like one of Elvis's famous rooms at Graceland I saw years later), a bong, wet bar and waterbed. Naturally that leveled up my respect for him.

One of the best aspects of working in the audio department was that contemporary (and mostly rock) music was playing all the time. One of the worst aspects was that I had to dress up for the work. My standard uniform, which I wear to this day, is a t-shirt and Levis, and a sweatshirt if I'm cold. I am rarely asked for fashion advice. So having to wear a tie (clip-on—again, that fashion advice situation), a button-down shirt, dress shoes and the worst, polyester dress pants, was stifling.

I was the guy sticking it to the man, remember? But now I resembled the man. But I did enjoy having some money for once, and even saved a little, perhaps three dollars, from my paltry wages. One of my great pleasures at that job was when I sold an item that had been languishing in the store for a long while, a high-end radio/cassette player, like a more modern CD-based Bose, but probably something like a Zenith back then.

That radio had been pointed out to me as having been on the shelves for months and months, and thus the boss had assigned a high SPIFF to it. Never having been a salesperson, a spiff sounded to me like a wet sneeze, but I was told it was a Sales Performance Incentive Funding Formula, which was muck-a-muck talk for a bonus given on the spot if you sold something.

When I sold that radio to an old man and made something like $40, all the other salespeople congratulated me in the way that said "Punk!" That was satisfying. Keep that up and I could make the Squareback into a love den like my colleague's.

But that was one of my few triumphs there. No wonder I had avoided jobs; my suspicions were all true—working was boring. Fluorescent lights, false friendliness, bad lunches and polyester. Ugh. I was so happy to come home and get out of those pants. But I was a lot happier when Zack came back. Zack left Canada with his hair on fire to get back to California, the day after he graduated from high school mid-1973.

Zack arrived, and we weren't sure what we were going to do. I remained that stalwart audio salesperson and model citizen. At some point, we started talking about buying a giant vehicle and traveling around in it. We went somewhere outside of LA and Zack drove a full-size for-sale school bus through the streets, which did raise my heartbeat, because it had a gamy transmission, and he'd never piloted a leviathan like that before.

But that beast was a faded mud puppy compared to the car we actually bought: a 1948 Dodge, a long, gigantic, black voluptuous thing with suicide doors and a massive steering wheel. In that marvelous marketing vernacular, it possessed something called "Fluid Drive," which allowed you to either drive away from a dead stop in high gear without using the clutch, or manually go clackety-clicking through the three gears on your way to its ponderous but satisfying top speed.

Fluid Drive was one of those confounded ideas that carries the kind of odd automotive charm that continued to pull me in later.

That Dodge was long ago, so the fact that we bought realistic-looking plastic machine guns to poke out of its big windows at startled passersby was funnier than it would be today, when someone might shoot back. But wheeling that massive black machine up and down the Pacific Coast Highway with the windows down gave me a taste for sensuous—if bulky—American steel, the giant steering wheel piloting a burly beast.

That wasn't long before Zack and I decided to get an apartment together, a little two-bedroom place in a small, ground-floor complex right next door to my sister Colleen's, who my father had kicked out because she was dating a Black guy. (My father still heard echoes of his Mississippi-born mother, who was sweet in many ways, but definitely unreconstructed.) The best part of the kick-out equation was that it was easier to bear living next to my oldest sister—who delighted in tormenting me and my brother—because the Black guy in question, Yogi, was living with her.

Yogi, who called me Tommy, because my sister still occasionally called me that from my boyhood, was a great guy. Big, handsome, friendly man with huge hands—he could roll a joint with one hand, which always impressed me. Zack and I could occasionally hear him singing to R&B from next door, where he could do a credible Marvin Gaye in a kind of high, sweet voice. We sometimes went over to their place and got high with him, and listened to records.

That he died in a cliffside fall in Mexico a couple of years later was a blow, and an earthquake to my sister. I wish I'd known him better, but I was honored to have been his friend. My sister would have a couple more earthquakes in her relationships to come.

But long before that, Zack and I had to figure out how to live in that apartment. At first we basically had no furniture, except for some stuff scrounged from my parents and my sister. We were sleeping in sleeping bags. We had an early run of luck when driving up one of the nearby big streets in the evening we saw a large couch sitting by the curb.

We managed to hoist that thing up on top of the giant Dodge (there must have been another person in the car, maybe Matt) balance it and get it to our house. It wasn't new, and was covered in some kind of dark, vinyl-like fabric, but it was in good shape. Indeed, this might have been someone's couch that they were moving into their apartment, went inside for a cup of coffee and came out and it was gone, but for us, it felt like fate.

It wasn't fate, but outright theft, that got us our prize pieces of furniture a little later. We had noticed, while driving around the new neighborhood, a used-car dealer, Osborne's, that had a couple of beautiful, restored vintage cars in their showroom. I think they sold all kinds of newer used cars, but those polished beauties drew people in.

Zack and I went to Osborne's several times and had some friendly chats with some salespeople, who liked our Dodge too. The Dodge was definitely not restored, but it was in OK shape and when you gave it a wash, it still sparkled. We'd go to

Osborne's once in a while, look at the cars, and leave. One time, late in an afternoon, we dropped by and there didn't seem to be anyone in the showroom.

We went in, and sat in, as we had before, these beautiful antique, wood and plush leather chairs they had there. These were big, heavy, handsome chairs with wide arms and fine leather seats. I don't know how it came to us, but we each took one of those chairs and brought them back to the Dodge and put them in the trunk.

The Dodge's trunk was cavernous, but these were very big chairs, so I think we had to tie the trunk lid down. That we got away with this was highly improbable, because the dealership was still open, and we could have easily been seen lugging these big chairs out of the showroom and putting them in our car.

That it was highly improbable was true; that it was highly unethical had to be as well. Again, I'd violated my "I'm sticking it to the man" rationalization, because we liked those people at Osborne's and they liked us. They weren't the man, they were just folks. But we stole their chairs.

That was the kind of theft opportunism I acted on a number of times. Grab now, consider later. I know I felt guilty about the Osbornes many times afterward, but I don't remember feeling lousy about it in the moment or soon afterward. I hope the better angels of my nature at least tugged at my conscience.

We managed to get some mattresses, but we either got them from friends or bought them, I don't remember. But with our big couch and chairs, we had the fundamentals for a living room. We started to get some visitors: Matt, Denny, Marty and even Joyce once in a while, who had befriended my old neighbor Janet from down the street in high school, and their deepening bond was good for me, because I remained pals with Janet from way back. I was still in the middle of screechingly breaking up with Lynn over the course of that year (perhaps once every two months or so), and still seeing Joyce as a friend. Naturally, I wanted to be friendlier.

Now that Zack was back in town, he being a party to and occasionally participant in my stealing, and we had a new base of operations, it was time to put things back in gear. Oh my, we went from first to third without bothering to stop at second.

I was still taking items from the various stores that had been so generous toward me in the past, but as I said, less so because I was working. But even with working, once I discovered that they were giving away liquor for free at this large market up the street from us, I landed my second job: liquor distributor.

My unwitting partner in this enterprise was the large liquor section of Boys Market, a big supermarket on busy Anaheim Street not far from our house. Boys was the nearest market of real size near our house, so at first it was our regular supermarket. But when I saw that walled-off liquor section (basically high walls on three sides), which was spacious and yet fundamentally concealed, I knew it was Christmas.

They had a plentiful array of half-pint bottles of every liquor known to man (no beast would have drunk our selections). They had some good liquor too. I still didn't quite have a grasp of the difference.

But I certainly had a grasp of the bottles. I still had that dependable corduroy coat from thievings past. Besides the record-theft slit I'd put in its liner, it also had the conventional inner pocket. That pocket was clearly designed by the manufacturer for slipping in half-pints of booze. I didn't even have to put any pressure on them under my arm. The pint bottles I did, because they wouldn't fit the pocket, but jacket-hidden pint bottles of liquor were old hat to me by then.

Zack and I were entertaining our old pals like Marty, Ron, Denny and Matt, plus occasional friends of theirs, girlfriends, state senators and the like at our home. Everyone enjoyed a drink, particularly because most of us were under 21. We often enjoyed a second drink as well. Thus I had a lot of work to do.

I was the most enthusiastic shopper: sometimes I would return to the store twice a day to continue canvassing for that subtle spirit that would best accompany our Cheetos. We drank intolerable things: raspberry brandy, sloe gin, and Pagan Pink Ripple wine that must have never known a grape. Many of those we drank in the name of science, since items like blueberry schnapps and MD—Mad Dog—20-20 "wine" surely weren't meant to be ingested—by humans at least. (You might think this diet would put someone in the hospital, but, in your late teen years, you aren't really a human being.)

Whoever designed those single-shot plastic bottles of booze that you see now at liquor counters surely didn't have a shoplifter in the family. They didn't exist in my heyday, but if they did, that would have been the proverbial "candy from a baby" situation. Those little envelopes of spirits looked like they were designed to be stolen. But I was busy enough then with your standard bottles.

We conducted other business from the house, often encouraged by our studious drinking. The building we were in had a ladder to the roof, which was flat with a low wall. We'd climb up there and watch the stars and dream. We'd also climb up there and watch the high school kids (well, let's be frank, we'd watch the girls more closely) from across the street in the day, because Wilson High, one of Long Beach's bigger high schools, was right across from our apartment complex.

When we weren't up on that roof musing on the state of the union, we were throwing water balloons at people on the street below. That this was probably not smart behavior was evidenced when we ballooned one of the high school's buses on the evening of a football game, and a couple of the football players came rampaging into the house. But this was when we had an advantage, because there were at least five dudes in the house, older than the football players, so all they did was yell a bit and leave. Probably they were scared off by my remarkable physique, which could be well likened to that of a pencil with a large, intimidating wig attached.

One of those Wilson football games was where I had one of my arrests, for the innocent joy of throwing firecrackers in a small crowd. Denny and I were cuffed from behind by a regular LB city cop with those vinyl cords they sometimes used rather than regular cuffs, but they released us at the station, so we were never actually booked on a disturbing-the-peace charge.

That incendiary moment paled next to one I authored in one of Marty's VW buses, when we were driving around and tossing firecrackers out of his car. However, we also had some M-80s as well. These were offhandedly called quarter-sticks of dynamite, which wasn't accurate, but they were considerably more powerful than a firecracker; they were allegedly used by the military to simulate explosives.

That they were also illegal of course made them more interesting to us. We could occasionally get M-80s and cherry bombs from Mexico, and when we could, we did. On this day, a number of us were in the van (perhaps Denny or Tom, Ron, Marty driving, maybe Matt) and I lit an M-80 and tried to throw it out of the window, but it hit the edge and bounced back in onto the floor of the van.

Panic! I shot back against the back seat, knocking Ron back in the process. That thing went off, and we discovered that a Volkswagen van is actually a reverberant sound chamber. An M-80 going off outside is very loud; one going off inside a VW van is thunderous. It felt catastrophic.

Marty was amazing. He didn't yell or accuse me of anything. He pulled over to the side of the road and we essentially fell out, I think onto grass, wherever we were. I could not hear at all, and could not begin to hear for several minutes. My head was hammering and pulsing—it felt like it was squeezing in and out. Everyone was holding their heads, sometimes talking loudly, because no one could hear.

Everyone agreed I was an asshole, and I had no argument. But no one really laid into me, which was gratifying. I have never lit an explosive device in a car again.

But I did get into people's mailboxes. This is one where you shake your head and think you'll load a grenade launcher in your mailbox to teach those damn kids a lesson. At one point sometime after we'd moved in to the apartment, a couple of us were out walking and I grabbed a bunch of mail out of someone's box a few blocks from our house. The stuff was mostly junk, but one envelope had a check made out for $125.00 to a woman I presume lived in the house. That wasn't a small amount of money to us.

This is how unsophisticated (besides idiotic) we were: I didn't have a bank account, but Denny did, and we signed the check with the woman's name and he deposited it into his account. And nothing happened. Except that the money was deposited.

How could that be? Why didn't someone trace the check, or question Denny as to why it was signed over to him? I don't know. We did it again after a couple of weeks (and this time instead of loutishly throwing away the other mail, we only took out what looked to be a check), for $80 for a male resident of our neighborhood. Same result: money, ours, prosecution, none.

We may have done the "Pay to the Order Of" legit statement for signing over checks to a third party, but I don't remember being that clever. Denny might have known how to do it, but maybe not. I'm happy we didn't attempt to steal mail again, because it once more confirmed to me that my alleged theft standards were made of melting ice, and couldn't withstand much scrutiny.

One of the more significant things I did after a few months at 10th Street was to quit my job as a department store salesperson. The work dulled my senses and my enthusiasm had been ebbing for some time. I can't remember if I immediately told my parents or not; I was still in fair contact, but probably waited a while to inform them. My father very much believed in the power of work. I had yet to show any belief.

I do remember one of my first acts, in the early evening of the day after I quit. I put my loathed black polyester pants on a stick and lit them on fire, and had a liberation parade on the street flanking our house, in front of the high school. If you have never lit polyester from the 1970s aflame, you wouldn't know that it would drip large globs of flaming plastic material as it burned, my Southern California version of napalm. I walked up and down the block with my pants on fire until little was left except cooling street globs and an inner glow of satisfaction.

Not long after that, Zack and I both got jobs as union pipe fitters at the Union Oil refinery in Wilmington, a little city north of Long Beach. A friend of Marty's got us the gig. Now, though Zack had some mechanical skills, I was about as suited to be a pipe fitter as a ballerina. However, one of the advantages of being in a union was that if there was something to be wrenched about, they'd send four or five people to the pipe: one of them to do the work, and the others would stand about bullshitting. I could do that.

Working in an oil refinery was a place where you didn't need to take acid to hallucinate. You'd wander through corridors of heated gases, surrounded by giant towers and stacks of metal and pipe. Strange screechings of metal and low thumping noises, damp fogs and smoke, and walkways where the air would be temperate and suddenly, 10 feet away, 25 degrees warmer. I got to carry a giant pipe wrench, which I don't think I ever used, but it was good exercise.

Weirdly enough, Joyce's dad was an executive at Union and I undoubtedly mentioned that I was working there around him, probably trying to make him believe that this unseemly mass of hair and bare feet lurking around his daughter was an actual person. But when rumors of a union strike started to circulate, he called me into the living room alone to have a manly talk with me, asking about the plans.

I wasn't as suspicious in those days as I am now, but from his questions I knew he wanted to me to rat out my union brothers (a deep brotherhood that I'd enjoyed a deep few weeks) and get the scoop on their plans. I stammered out a bunch of crap about how I didn't know the details (and I really didn't, even though Zack and I had attended at least one meeting), and he let me go with the warning to let him know when anything was up.

They did indeed go on strike some weeks later, and I wasn't invited back on the job. They probably blackballed me for being a snitch, though I'd held true. Zack might have worked there longer than me; that detail is lost in the oily smoke of those days. And I still continued to visit Joyce, to play Frisbee with her, to ride bikes with her, and to lust, to no avail. I was still with Lynn, and that would be the case for a bit to come. I would have liked the oil company to have awarded me one of those pipe wrenches so I could melt it down and build a car, but alas.

Zack and I did want to have a Christmas at our place, but money was always tight. But you can't have Christmas without a tree, correct? There was a Christmas tree lot not far from our house that was surrounded by eight-foot chain-link fences. But a week before Christmas, in the evening, we climbed up on the fence and used a rope to lasso a close Christmas tree, and pulled the damn thing over. It was too tall for our ceiling, so we trimmed it to fit.

Colleen had moved out by then, and our new neighbors were a ponytailed "groovy" dad and his 10-year-old daughter. The dad had a huge hookah, perhaps four-feet tall with a big brass bowl that he'd fill with pot. We joined him a couple of times, since the hookah had six hoses attached.

His daughter was one of those impossibly cute and sassily precocious kids that are a specialty on television now. She would come over and harass us and try to prove how casually smart she was. Very close to Christmas, Zack walked into our apartment after us both being gone, and she was on the floor, surrounded by our Christmas presents that she was unwrapping.

She apologized, but was undaunted. She likely would have made a fine shoplifter. She probably married a Monte Carlo playboy and gave him heartburn for the rest of his days.

Speaking of impressionable kids, I must relate one of those simple twists of fate that happened during this time that might have prompted "Well, that was weird" at the moment of their occurrence, but then give you a serious shiver and chill years later. Rick was down visiting from his Army posting in Monterey. Denny had seen a poster that had a bunch of spiritual gobbledygook on it, suggesting a lecture where your hidden potentials and power could be pulled out.

Den has always liked some good spiritual gobbledygook, and he convinced us to drive down south to a community college, maybe in Costa Mesa or Santa Ana, where these two lecturers were presenting their spiel. There were two presenters, an older man and woman, who discussed cosmic enlightenment, freedom from the shackles of the body, and other topics that go best after smoking a large joint.

At the end of the presentation, which was well attended, mostly by college-age folks, they suggested that everyone in the room go with them, then and there, to a retreat in Oregon. No details on how we would be housed or what would happen, just that this was the opportunity to get on board.

Dennis, who was known to be a spontaneous sort, was into it—why not? Rick was still in the Army, and not ready to go AWOL, and I was still partially sane, so none of us did it.

We later found out that the presenters were known as Bo and Peep, and also "The Two." They gained no small notoriety by founding an organization of true believers known as Heaven's Gate just a year or two later. In March of 1997, the bodies of 39 members of the cult (including "Bo," Marshall Applewhite), clad in new Nikes and draped with purple cloths, were found dead, part of a ritual suicide. They were going to meet a spacecraft, the mothership, that was to appear along with the Hale-Bopp comet.

I was happy to have not ridden that spacecraft.

There were more benign, if lackluster, comets than Hale-Bopp. Late in the year, just after Christmas, a bunch of us gathered on the roof, for at least a couple of evenings in a row, for the heralded passing of the comet Kohoutek, which was allegedly going to emblazon the sky with an incandescent trail. But the only thing lit on the roof was us, fully lubricated with a lot of my ill-gotten spirits from Boys Market. I've seen better barbecue lightings than Kohoutek's flame.

But just a couple of nights later, on New Year's Eve, there were some real fireworks.

CHAPTER ELEVEN

New Year's Crimes and Doing the Time

Some nights, if you are lucky (?) enough, you get a glimpse of what prompted Rod Serling to create "The Twilight Zone." New Year's Eve, 1973, was such a night. Though perhaps the *Animal House* version of the Twilight Zone is more accurate. Zack and I had now been on 10th street for four or five months, on our own for really the first time. This was our first New Year's together as that eager, barely tolerable species: swinging apartment-dweller-type guys, barely out of high school. We were going to celebrate that self-congratulatory state of being with a New Year's party.

That evening we had a respectable turnout of our friends, acquaintances and other welfare cheats of note, and had settled in to the numerous foolishnesses of New Year's Eve. As it neared midnight, Zack and I had an *insight:* we could both doff our clothes and walk around outside in the soft warm rain that was falling to christen the New Year. Did I mention we'd had a drink or two?

Equally inspired, my girlfriend Lynn and our pal Ron decided to join us. We goofed around a bit out front, and then we saw two figures approaching up the block. In the great spirit of improvisation, Zack and I worked up a plan: we would walk up to the people, acting as though we were in our fully clothed at-ease, and wish them Happy New Year's. Ah, the inspired, spontaneous act of creation.

Remember, it was dark and misting outside. Thus you can understand that it wasn't until we were but five feet away from our prey and about to spring our greeting when we realized it was OUR LANDLORD AND LANDLADY, who lived only a few blocks away, and who had decided to walk over and wish us happy New Year's. The fact that they were very straight-laced, reserved people, and Eastern Europeans yet, made our calculation all the less calculating.

Well. We had perfect presence of mind and body: Run! Without saying a word, we turned and bolted for the house. Somebody at the party, I think Matt, caught a classic picture of Zack in manic bare-to-the-bone retreat into the house, eyes bulging out of his head like boiled eggs. Perhaps we thought we'd be safe inside. I actually ran into my closet and hid, lacking the benefit of clothing. I can blame it on the liquor and youth, but poor decision-making seemed to be a consistent theme those days.

So, the party was in full bloom while we're all running in, screaming that the landlord was outside. We actually locked the door on him. One truly funny thing was that his wife's full focus of outrage targeted only Lynn alone. We could hear my landlady shouting, "Naked women in streets! Naked women in streets!" over and over. What really caught our attention was our landlord, though, who shouted even louder, "All right, dammit, that's it. The cops are going to be here in five minutes.

You're all in big trouble!" After his shouting of a few more epithets, they left.

All hell broke loose inside. We were in a rare state of intoxication, euphoria, fear, confusion and glory. We all decided to leave, immediately. The naked perpetrators flung on clothes. I decided to stay over at Lynn's house: she still lived with her mom, and we jumped in her mom's Karmann Ghia, a nice little car I often drove. Many cars were leaving at once, in a crazed caravan.

Remember that nice, soft rain I mentioned? Well, it hadn't rained for a while before this, and the streets were slick—and so was my thinking. I was behind one of our friend's cars, and when he stopped at the first stop sign near our house, I plowed right into the back of his car. His car was unscathed. The Ghia, though, had the impact resistance of a tortilla chip. I walloped the front end, pushing one of the fenders against the wheel so that it made a horrific noise while we drove.

And drive we did, because we didn't know what else to do. Continuing back to my girlfriend's house, stopped at a traffic signal, I looked over at the driver next to us. Do you know that "Twilight Zone" episode where William Shatner sees the ominous yeti-like figure on the wing of his plane, and he realizes he's doomed? Well, that same beast was staring at me from his next-lane car window. I still don't know if he was wearing a horrific mask or if it was some poor, deformed curiosity seeker, but seeing that possessed werewolf seemed to seal the evening.

The Ghia was considered a total loss by the insurance company; Lynn's mom resented me for it to the end of her days. When we went back to our apartment the next afternoon, we found our landlord's note on the door telling us we had until the end of the weekend to get out of the apartment. We didn't know anything about rental laws, and we meekly complied. Zack and I (and perhaps Ron) spent the next three nights rusticating in a nearby public park in sleeping bags before we found a new place. Lucky that Southern California is temperate in the winters. It was sort of like camping, but because we had no choice in the matter, it was like camping in a dank basement. Happy New Year.

Zack and Ron and I moved into a small house in the lower regions of Signal Hill, the small hilltop city—though it was a city in miniature—completely surrounded by Long Beach proper. We brought the Osborne chairs and our big couch and our '48 Dodge and Zack's 60s International Travelall.

Signal Hill still displayed active elements of its oil-industry history: There were many patches of working oil wells toward the top of the hill, their massive triangular grasshopper heads pumping steadily up and down to draw up the black gold, as they had for many years. More than once after we moved in we went out at night and climbed up on those things, riding the slow motion of the beast's long neck, and getting oiled-up clothes in the process.

That might not seem to have been a sensible thing to do, but we did it. But we did much more nefarious things. I continued to orchestrate liquor distribution from various stores, including Boys Market, such a generous supplier of goods. I'd begun to feel impervious to capture, so that I would walk around the market before I did my shopping, eating things like full packages of cinnamon rolls right out of the box. Sugar still drove many of my moods.

One of the streets that flanked our neighborhood was a spot for truckers to park their rigs overnight. Because of the gas crisis, people were more and more putting locking gas caps on their cars, the punks. But most commercial trucks (non-diesel) didn't have those then, so for a while we used a 5-gallon gas can to dip into their tanks. But that was too heavy to lug back up to our house, and 1-gallon cans too inefficient, so we only did that a couple of times.

What I also did with Tom only a couple of times was one of those "man, that's cold!" acts that brings red to my cheeks. I'd told you before that Tom was a skilled mechanic, and that he owned Volkswagens, often several at a time, sprucing them up for sale. On a couple of nights on the Hill we stole VW carburetors right out of people's cars. Well, I basically handed him the tools while he wrenched off the carburetors, because he had the skills. We stole a set of nice baby moon hubcaps off a VW bug as well one time.

There's no justification for that—I won't even try. And I'd had the existence of hell mentioned to me a thousand or more times in my early schooldays. Kids, they just don't listen.

I've told you I was getting pretty cocky about my booze boosting and well, boosting in general. The universe decided to teach me a lesson. We had a new house, but I had my old habits: again, I continued lifting things that weren't mine out of stores, and continued going to Boys Market to replenish our liquor holds, which had to take care of the thirsts of many pals who stopped by, like Denny, Marty and Matt and pals of their pals and pals of everyone's pals. It had been some time since I'd had any contact with authority figures over my thieving, and I thought the good times wouldn't end.

But my liquid empire turned into broken glass at Boys Market the day I went in with an order for a half-pint of Chivas Regal for Marty. (We clearly were getting snooty about our tippling.) Getting uppity was obviously my undoing—I should have stuck with peach schnapps. Half-pints were cake, so I breezed out the door thinking my usual delicate thoughts when a plain-clothes officer touched my shoulder. This time, because another confederate of his was in front of me, I didn't throw my goods at him and didn't run. I meekly surrendered, the cops were called, and they took me down.

Get popped before you're 18, you go down to juvenile hall for a few hours, and you get a misdemeanor that's later wiped from your record. Go down at 19, it's a different story—depending on the charge and circumstances, you can spend a little time in the clink and get a mark on your record that sticks. I was brought in a squad car to the Long Beach jail downtown and booked. Bail was set at $500.

This extraordinary miscarriage of justice occurred on a Friday in the early afternoon. My friends, none of whom had other than pocket cash at the time, assembled their pink slips and went to a bail bondsman. We're a little sketchy on the history here, but I believe it was four cars (definitely the '48 Dodge and Marty's '66 VW bus, Zack's 60s International Travelall, and I think my '64 VW Squareback) that were put up as collateral.

And turned down. I would have enjoyed seeing the bail-bonds person roll their eyes at the list. We should have offered them the Osborne chairs.

Our taste in cars was as fine as our taste in liquor. High living it wasn't. Because it was the weekend and bail could only be rendered on the weekdays, I was shut out: though I'd been in a jail cell a few times, those glories were only for an hour or two. Here, I had time to get comfy.

I did learn some things, because jail was an education.

I didn't know that they intended a person to actually sleep on a mattress that was two inches high, adorned with a thin wool Army blanket. I didn't know that you could have a weird, integrated steel unit, a hybrid toilet/sink/drinking fountain in a cell, and how unappealing taking a drink from it would be. I didn't know in city jail you could have a cellmate who would spend HOURS talking about the thousands of women he had slept with, and how grateful they were for his talents.

I didn't know you could be fed three meals a day, all of which seemed to have one or more elements covered in a shiny kind of slime. (What *was* that?) I didn't know that we would be allowed into a kind of inner courtyard shared by all the unit's cells for a couple of hours a day, and that someone would go nuts, attack some other dude with a spoon and have to be beaten down by a guard in front of us all.

I learned those things, but I probably had a learning disability: after I got out, though not immediately, I did steal more things. Some of those thefts were quite intriguing, as you'll find out. But it was more for old time's sake. But as a generality, there was a significant curtailing of my pilferage—or plans of pilferage. I didn't scan for opportunities with the avidity I once had.

After thieving had become second nature to me, as I suggested earlier, I'd enter a store, a store of any kind, and look around to see the security, the placement of wares, the doors. I convinced myself that my fingers actually tingled when I cased a joint. But after jail, the thrill was gone—my tingling tapered off.

There would be a modest resurgence, but that was some time later. In the meantime, we'd been on Signal Hill for a few months, and everyone was a bit restless. I was getting unemployment for my Zody's job, so I had a small amount of money. My friend Denny had chased a woman up to Seattle (he does claim he was invited), because he was the chasing kind, stayed with her a bit, and then took an apartment in a suburb there. I was still able to collect California unemployment, and could pretend to look for work in Washington rather than pretend in California, so I traveled up.

When I got to Dennis' one-bedroom apartment, he had added an additional roommate, Brian. Because Dennis had to go back to Southern California for something about a week after I arrived, he left me with Brian. I soon learned that Brian was unusual. Brian and I never did any shoplifting, but I must spend a bit of time discussing our relationship, because it too was unusual.

Though he was in his mid-thirties, Brian sometimes looked like a little lost boy, sometimes a fragile old man. He was of average height, soft in the belly, with a wide face, big red lips, and wispy, blondish-white hair that he wore long and scraggly.

Brian was morbidly pale, almost ghoulish, with great dark circles under his eyes. He also had an odd manner, almost preternaturally calm, talking—from the moment I met him—in a slow, modulated, recitation-style way.

Brian had been institutionalized for some instability years before. He did have some medication to help: pills, lots of pills. I'm not talking about aspirin here—these were serious psychoactive products: Thorazine, Librium, Tofranil, Lithium, bottles and bottles and bottles, and I saw him occasionally mix up a bunch—without looking at the labels—and take them all. But he hardly ever acted differently from how he always acted: slow, agreeable, and odd.

Equally odd were his habits with his cigarettes. Every morning, he used a rolling machine to manufacture his cigarette cache. Our first morning, he plopped down at the table and proceeded to roll cigarettes like a madman, a crazed, living tobacco factory, for over an hour.

The table was soon piled with misshapen little sticks. I learned that this was how he began every morning. I also learned that he would put a cigarette in his mouth and light it the second, the very *second,* he woke up. I later found these ugly, half-smoked cigarettes on the edge of the sink, on the saucers under plants, everywhere, soggy and brown, disgusting slimy little slugs.

Brian told me many peculiar things, almost always weirdly sexual. Once he turned to me and said, "My teeth weren't always like this." (He had these dark gray stains on all his teeth near the gums.) "My teeth were fine until a few years ago, but I ate out this nasty girl, just really nasty, and the next day they were like this." I started to laugh until I saw him smiling calmly at me, displaying the evidence of how a woman had wronged him.

Another time he told me he had had an erection for 72 hours, and that ever since his sperm had been thin and milky when he masturbated. I told him that with all the pills he ate, he was lucky that his sperm wasn't green, but he insisted it was due to chemicals in processed foods, most likely breakfast cereals.

Brian's dietary habits were unique: he opened cans of soup, put a spoon in them, and then left them in the refrigerator to be eaten later. The first time I saw him do this, I thought it was a joke. When I asked him about it, he just shrugged, and in that maddeningly placid way of his, said that he "liked it." I tried to understand, but I was raised in the suburbs; it seemed to be a crime against nature.

But for me, Brian's greatest crime was the fact that he would bring young girls—and I was 19, but these were girls years younger than me—home, and apparently have sex—or something—with them. It killed me that Brian, a guy that I thought had the sex appeal of a germ, had something going for him with girls. I'm not referring to wretched, sleazebag queens either—these were nice, wholesome-looking young women who seemed friendly and aware. I sat in Seattle for months without as much as a woman's phone number, and once every couple of weeks Brian would bring in one of his conquests.

Brian met these victims on his drives. He went for drives every day. Long drives, hours long. He didn't really go any-where, just the parks, the pretty places on the Sound, the wooded roads, sometimes through the city. He just didn't stop, unless he needed gas. The first couple of weeks we lived to-gether he'd say he was going out for a drive, and I'd ask where and he'd say, "No place in particular." Every time, "No place in particular."

He told me that he often picked up girls when they were hitchhiking. This was a time when it wasn't too unusual to see girls hitchhiking alone or in pairs. Mothers, the word's already gotten out, but in case you haven't heard, there are Brians out on the highway looking for your daughters.

Luckily, before I was inculcated into Brian's cult, I headed over to Wenatchee, in central Washington, where my old high school pal Ron was working on an apple orchard. Ron had headed for the hills from Long Beach from our place in Signal Hill the summer before, rather than to the drizzly-damp streets of Seattle. I don't know where Ron got the idea to go up to the apple orchards of central Washington to work, but that's what he did. That decision would affect many of my friends' lives and mine for years afterward.

That apple orchard in Wenatchee, the Keller ranch, became for us one of those power spots fabled by seers and mystics, seeking places of energy and spiritual solace. And in addition, in our cases, places of pot smoking, apple fights, dubious hygiene, and the kind of weary bliss that occurred after working 10- to 12-hour days in the hot sun and flopping on the cooling ground to watch blazing sunsets. Oh, there was some thieving too.

Power spots draw seekers, and thus they came: Zack back up from Southern California, Denny over from Seattle, Debbie, Zack's pal (and all of ours as well) from Vancouver, who had visited us at our 10th Street apartment in Long Beach and had gained my deepest respect by nearly finishing a gallon of what some absurdist vendor had labeled "wine," and in a marathon day of wine drinking, had fallen asleep with her arms affectionately around the toilet in our bathroom.

Marty came to pick as well, as did for a time, Joe, our high school Deadhead friend. Brent, Zack's other best pal from Vancouver, who became a good friend of all of our group, came by for a round of laughs. Kim, from Seattle, who became an honored member of our tribe, Andrea—all made the amiable orchard rounds.

We met Gonzalo, who already knew a thing or two (or a thousand) about apple picking, as well as about guitar picking and homespun philosophizing, which was a very valuable talent on a deep orchard evening.

The orchard was settled on a hillside above the town, and directly east was Saddle Rock, a humped prominence on one of the low, surrounding mountains. The folds of the "saddle" made a soft "V" in which the harvest sun rose. The magenta rays streaming down the dry, dun-colored hillsides were always a lovely sight at six in the morning, even when you knew you were in for a day's labor.

The orchard was perhaps fifty or sixty acres, predominantly Red Delicious and McIntosh, with Goldens and pears and a couple of bounteous cherry trees as well. It was owned by a gentle giant, Rod Keller, who could carry two 14-foot ladders at a time like they were rakes.

The grounds were mostly flat, with a few gradual rises, and a couple of strong hills that could be hell on inexperienced pickers who didn't know how to set a tall ladder in a tree on an incline. One time I was reaching out for a lone apple on a long branch and I fell from near the top of my ladder directly down into a bin two-thirds full of apples onto my back. Apples are not soft—I'm not sure who or what was more bruised.

We lived in crude cabins, with wood-burning stoves, sleeping in old beds, waking up at 6 to work 10-hour days picking apples. It was real labor, but it was good to be in the hillside trees looking out to Saddle Mountain, good to eat the fresh apples, good to be with my pals, good to drink cheap beer at night. Working all day in the hot sun, peeping out at your fellows through the green leaves, taking a long shower to scour off the day's sweat-stuck dirt—that was good.

But that didn't keep me from getting up to some no-good in Wenatchee. A guy had to stay in practice. First, a prelude: Long Beach was home to Cal State University Long Beach, which was only a mile and a half or so from my house. As teens we used to play pickup baseball on its fields in the summers and basketball in the fall. But those innocent pursuits were matched by the time we spent messing around on the campus, on weekends when most of the buildings were shut down.

But not locked.

We'd walk through the hallways of the various campus buildings and try doors at random. Most of them were sensibly locked, but once in a while they weren't. I remember doing this the most with Zack, me probably 14 and him 13. So, we'd occasionally open a professor's door and look in their drawers and at what was on their shelves, or we'd get into some kind of storage shed and see if there was anything to mess around with. I don't remember actually stealing things from the school, but I don't remember not stealing things.

But that testing-the-door for security became a thing I did almost automatically from that point on, in all kinds of buildings. That's why one evening when we were out buying some groceries from one of the local Wenatchee stores, I tried the back-alley door of local Greyhound station. Bingo!

This was the old-school kind of Greyhound station, with a cafe, stools at the counter, a beat-up old waiting room. I can't fully remember who I was with; one might have been Ron, because he was our lead guy in town, having spent time there the summer before; pretty sure Debbie was there too. But we went into the pantry area and saw some familiar staples: Corn flakes and other cereals, rice and canned goods, and a fridge full of cooler items. I took a case of canned tuna, a case of those tiny boxes of cereal—the ones you split down the middle and pour the milk into the box—and a gallon of milk.

I'm not sure what my companions took. We were able to get the stuff back to the orchard with my car, the sturdy 36-horsepower 1959 Volkswagen bug, that happened to have a big, faded Tweety Bird painted on the driver's side door.

We tried this again two weeks later and the door was—magic!—still unlocked. They had some kind of counter desserts in a case, like donuts or pastries, and I took a bunch of those, as well as some other canned goods, a case of Budweiser that I hadn't seen before and the crowning jewel, a full ham from the fridge. Of course we had to try it again sometime later, but the third time was charmless; someone had learned to turn the lock. I probably should have been recognized by the town council for sacrificing my own body—sparing the public the donuts—for the sake of the health of weary travelers, but the recognition never came.

We sometimes would stay up on the orchard for a week or more without going into town—why bother, when it was a kind of sylvan paradise? The only other thing of consequence I remember stealing in Wenatchee was an American flag on the Fourth of July that was hanging on the outside wall of one of the downtown businesses. This was a clear crime, particularly in a small, rural Americana-like town, so I probably would have been summarily executed had I been caught.

But I wasn't caught. Instead, because I was a long-legged lad, and the cab of a '59 Volkswagen is very small and mine happened to have a ragtop sunroof that pulled all the way back over the back seat, I could sit propped up, butt near the top of the driver's seat, head out of the sunroof and still manage to push in the clutch and shift gears. As good Americans, we had been drinking that 4th of July day in Wenatchee, so we rolled merrily through the town and around the various orchards, me with my head out the top of the car and the American flag waving, patriots all.

Apple picking usually begins in late August in Washington and can easily last into October, depending on the size of the orchard, its location and the types of apples. And there can be weeks of prep work too, like propping up the laden branches with long poles called, duh, props. We'd been there a couple of weeks when Lynn showed up.

I should have mentioned this earlier: I'd said that Lynn and I had been going through a tumultuous time in the last year or so of our relationship. There were many loud exchanges, many stormings out, many breakups. A memorable moment occurred when I dashed out of her house in Long Beach and got in the '48 Dodge and started driving away and Lynn grabbed the outside door handle and was dragged along for ten feet or so, with her mother at her door screaming "My daughter, my daughter!"

But we finally had broken up some months before I went to Washington. And Joyce and I had gotten together. That had taken some persuading.

Though Joyce and I had spent a good deal of time together, and had had a great deal of fun and had enjoyed each other's company, she wasn't shopping for a boyfriend. She didn't even seem to glance at the boyfriend shelves, which of course inspired me all the more. She also wasn't thrilled with the extended mad hatter's behavior of my relationship with Lynn, which I didn't talk about too much.

But after Lynn and I seemed to have actually broken up (with all the shattered emotional glass therein), Joyce made me the saddest man in the world, after I asked her for us to be together: "No, I don't want a boyfriend." The next day, she called me to make me the happiest man in the world by saying, "OK."

And it was way better than OK.

So when Lynn showed up at the orchard, uninvited, that cast a pall. But much deeper darkness was to come, when within the day I was having sex with Lynn. Now Catholic boys are no slouches in the guilt department, but even with that wave of shame, I still had sex with her a couple of other times during her short stay there.

She wasn't there to pick apples; she was there to pick me apart, and I helped. I was a cloudy-skulled participant in my own undoing. At the end of the harvest, I picked a final apple from my final tree, and mailed it to Joyce. I probably didn't consider any Garden of Eden parallels. Many months later, I told Joyce about the betrayal and she was stunned and hurt, but we never spoke about it at length.

Again, my ignorance of the right thing to do stings, even now. I was so thrilled to have Joyce finally become part of my life in an intimate and joyful way, and I threw that in her face with a couple of sweaty romps in an old cabin in an apple orchard. Was that worth it? Hell no, as my father would say.

It was almost two full years later before Joyce and I actually broke up; we had many good times to come, but that faithlessness left a shadow. I regained some of her trust, but our connection would never be the same. After a while, I moved north to Sonoma County for college, and she was in Southern California, where we were trying to have a long-distance relationship. We wrote and saw each other on occasional long weekends, but when I got the inevitable "Dear XXX" letter, I wasn't that surprised.

I remember a line from the letter: She said she had felt for the longest time that I was merely "floating on the surface," a sham of sorts, a person without depth. The acuity of that tossed-off remark pierced me like an arrow. She said, after all this time, that she didn't really know me. I had no real answer.

She then had a college boyfriend for a couple of years. Later, she took up with an adventurer, a fellow photographer, with whom she deeply connected. They lived together for a bit, and then in the early 80s decided to go on a photographic jaunt down an obscure river in Columbia. They disappeared, and were never found, despite repeated visits there by both sets of parents.

I was living in Seattle when Janet sent me a newspaper clipping of the story of her disappearance. Janet was someone I would eagerly grill when I saw her: "How's Joyce? Is she still with that guy? Does she seem happy?" Though I'd been in a few relationships since our breakup, Joyce was still the woman I loved. Reflecting on the course of our relationship had never felt like an ignorant obsession with me; I felt her to be my soulmate, and that I'd asininely squandered something precious. I forever regret never fully telling her how much she meant to me.

But back then, feeling guilty, yes, but with the glow of a harvest season in the apple orchard, I still thought things were looking up.

Nixon had resigned. Not until Trump had there been a more criminal president. The world again felt open.

It wasn't clear what the future would hold, but even after my jail stint, I thought I could steal at least a part of it.

CHAPTER TWELVE

Yes More Pencils, Yes More Books

I returned to Seattle after the apple harvest in the middle of the fall, in time to drive with Denny to the Spokane Expo '74, which was the first environmentally themed World's Fair (and also where the IMAX theater had its debut). The drive to Spokane from Seattle is four hours, long enough for us to plot a misdeed.

Even though the admission was only five bucks or so, we were so enthusiastic about getting away with something that we scaled a fence and dropped into the huge fairgrounds, true daredevils. And though there were all kinds of exhibits, rides, musical events and fanfare, I don't remember much about the event, other than the fact we didn't pay.

I do know we rambled through the grounds and gaped at the scene; I dimly remember that Spokane Falls, powered by the rushing Spokane River, was part of that scene. And even if we did eat any sausages at the Bavarian Beer Garden, we didn't throw the wrappers on the ground—we were environmentalists, after all.

Back in Seattle, prospects were slim. Since I was on the short side of mediocre as an apple picker, I hadn't lined my pockets with much more than stems. My unemployment had run out a while before. Skies were darkening for winter. (Well, that's poetic license: skies in Seattle can darken any damn time of the year.)

I missed Joyce, I missed being barefoot, maybe I even missed some semblance of order in my life. And I'm unsure why they took me back in, other than I was always good with cleaning up my room (perhaps the better to hide things in), but my parents agreed to let the prodigal return.

Turn the calendar pages (think of your favorite black and white movie from the 50s) to the beginning of 1975. Rick was up in Seattle, possibly at the beginning of his post office career, and moving further into his relationship with his wife-to-be, Cindy, who was more interesting than sorting mail.

Despite my efforts to avoid it, I decided, perhaps with my mother's nudging, to go back to school. Not having a job might have been an influence. Long Beach had and still has a good community college, Long Beach City College, and there I reclaimed my scholarly ways. For a semester, at least.

I followed that spring semester with a fall semester at Cal State Long Beach, the sprawling campus an easy walk or bike ride away from my house. I made moderate efforts with my schoolwork, likely because I wasn't creative enough to design opportunities for trouble. Zack stayed in Seattle for a bit and then headed back to British Columbia to work on the railroad with Brent. Denny and Matt were also ensconced in Seattle. Ron remained in central Washington in the orchards, where he continued to work for a few years. Many of my old orchard pals and I did some picking stints at his new orchard in beautiful Lake Chelan, not far from Wenatchee, in '75 and '76.

Ron came back to Long Beach after a while, bummed around some, and ended up working as the general maintenance guy for his older brother, who'd become somewhat of a slumlord for some apartment properties in the less prosperous areas of Long Beach. I saw Ron infrequently when I'd come home from school and later from other places I lived over time. I saw him less over the years.

He'd taken on a veneer of being kind of a tough guy, which if you knew him, was just a protective mechanism. He'd been bullied or dismissed a lot in his life, and that had made him more cynical and wary. I mentioned earlier how I'd become a Jesus Freak for a period in high school: because Ron had always wanted to be a part of something, he joined me at a number of evangelical gatherings. At one, he was surrounded by young Christians, four or five, who almost maniacally insisted he speak in tongues to declare his love and connection to the Lord.

Ron was completely out of his element, uncomfortable and anxious, and finally, after their insistent entreaties went up another notch on the scale, he bleated out an incantation of nonsense words and splutters, and they all hugged him. Even God bullied Ron.

His real self had always been open, and fun and goofy, but in his later days, that was covered by new, more brittle layers. I wish I'd given him more of the love he craved. He died of pancreatic cancer near his birthday in 2007, at 53. At least I spoke to him on the phone at the hospital the evening before, and told him I loved him.

Back to my own Long Beach past: I wasn't going to steal liquor and drink it in my room at home, and none of my cronies were around to dare me to steal something. So my only ventures into theft came out of longing: Joyce had enrolled at the university in Santa Barbara, and though she came home on random weekends, that wasn't enough.

So, on several occasions, I stole my parents' car and drove it up there. How does a newish Ford Maverick, my parents' only car, disappear without notice? Easy: I stole it after they went to bed, drove the two hours to Santa Barbara, spent a few hours with Joyce in her dorm apartment (she had at least two roommates, so we hung out in the living room) and drove back the same night.

Now, I was 19, so as well as being an idiot, I had some stamina, but that was a taxing drive. I usually got home around 4am or so, but one time I arrived back at 5:25 and just got the garage door down on the car and entered the house heading to my room, only to meet my father coming into the kitchen at 5:30.

I mentioned that my father worked at Ford for nearly 40 years—he probably missed three days of work in his life, and had been getting up at 5:30am for years. He was sleepy, walking in to get a drink of water, and said to me, "Tommy, what are you doing up?"

I mumbled something about not being able to sleep, but said I was going back to bed, even though I was fully clothed, and even had a jacket on. I went to my room, thinking my dad would surely know I'd driven the car, because it had to still be warm when he went out to drive to work.

But he never said a word. Not long after that, I pegged the driver's side door panel of that Maverick on a nearby freeway-ramp entrance guard rail while rounding the corner at speed, which tore a wedge into the door. That was during a sanctioned use of the car, but that didn't put me in good stead as a driver in the Bentley household.

I still went to Santa Barbara occasionally, but by bus. In the meantime, I was restless. School had been OK, but just OK. Zack came back to California, restless himself. What do two restless lads do? Road trip.

We bought Matt's parents' gigantic '66 Dodge Polara station wagon, which rivaled our old '48 Dodge in length, though not in style. But it had a big, gas-sucking V8 that would push that thing plungingly forward, despite its bulk. And the passenger seats folded down, so we could easily sleep in the back of the thing. We called it the Dodge Hotel, and we were off.

It was moving in on winter, but winter in Southern California is often just a cooler version of summer. In parts of Northern California, winter is more like winter, though a Vermonter would just laugh. We had sleeping bags, an extra blanket, canned goods, a cooler, some bits of camping stuff and good intentions.

We didn't have much dough, but Zack and I had traveled in that condition before. We figured we could stop in some of the bigger cities, find work for a while, and either stay for a stretch or move on. Despite being ultra-professional refinery workers and apple pickers, we couldn't find work the whole length of California, mostly because the refineries were all down south, and any apples had already been picked that season.

So we decided to continue north to Oregon, though we had to do some shopping first. I mentioned the cooler weather in Northern California. The nights in the back of Dodge were getting quite crisp, so that our fundamentally gunny-sack sleeping bags had lost their courage. We also didn't have much in the way of camp goods to cook with, and couldn't afford restaurants.

Thus, we stopped in at a large department store that had camping equipment. I had a minor Renaissance of my old days of walking out of stores carrying briefcases or dribbling basketballs: I walked out of that store with a large, completely unfurled down sleeping bag, one that could be unzipped and thrown over the both of us. Zack carried out at least one of those nested aluminum camp kits, where there's a saucepan with a folding handle, bowls and cups.

When we were getting ready to walk out I said something to him like, "You're a ghost; no one can see you." It had always worked for me. It worked this time too. Somewhere also along the lines we took a couple of gallons of milk to go along with the car's supply of cereal from a loading dock in a warehouse district, where I think we were looking for work. Beggars can't be choosers, but they can be thieves.

As for real work, there wasn't much. We hung out for several days in soggy Eugene, hoping to pick up some labor on a Hoedad crew. The Hoedads were a cooperative tree-planting organization that gained some fame in that time, and for a time to come. They were known for their progressive ideas and ideals.

They were also known for hard work on slick slopes in Oregon woods. They called themselves "hoedads" because the main tree-planting tool was a hoe-like implement. Now, since Zack and I had spent summers and falls picking apples in the Wenatchee hills, we thought we had an idea of what rural work was like and what rural workers were like.

In Wenatchee, we worked with people who didn't give a damn if the worms were in the apples or in their hair. We worked with a guy named Scotty whose last bath had to have been in the sink just after the wolf gave birth to him. We were used to being dirty ourselves, but my, wasn't a shower nice after a 10-hour shift?

But we lingered around the Hoedads office for days, our names on the signup sheets, but we were never called. We saw some tough, dirt-caked characters come in and out of that office, muscles bulging and eyes glazed. And those were the women. The men were more of the Neanderthal type, but better at rolling joints. Both Zack and I had long hair and beards too, but we probably seemed like we'd just come from day-care.

We left Eugene and started to head up to Portland, but our enthusiasm was waning. It can be mighty rainy in those parts too, and that can dampen the spirits. What to do? Best to take all of your skills and motivations and rely on a trick that job hunters have used since time immemorial: nepotism.

My sister Colleen had met a nice fellow named Terry, and he'd been promoted to be the head of UPS for southern Nevada. There ain't all that many bodies in southern Nevada (live ones at least), but a lot of them are clustered in Vegas and surrounds. Colleen and Terry had moved into a fairly big house in Vegas.

I did say Terry was a nice fellow, and he was, but he seemed way too straight for my sister, and had a kind of hail-fellow-well-met salesperson's personality, at least to me. But goodness, he would turn out to be not that straight—not by a long shot.

We talked to Colleen on the phone from somewhere in Oregon, and after conferring with Terry, he told her he could get us jobs at UPS. He didn't have to ask anyone—he was the boss. So, Vegas it was. Having stayed in Vegas what seemed to be a thousand times with my parents (and a few times as an adult), the notion seemed fine to me, and to Zack as well.

I then took on one of my odder jobs: Bad Address Clerk. Because Vegas is a town of drifters, grifters and shifters of identity, packages would continually go astray, paralleled by the wanderings of their addressees, who in a month's time in Vegas might have changed their residence—and their jobs, spouses and perhaps even their sex—two or three times. And then disappeared. So my shelves were filled with boxes large and small, for which the drivers could find no recipients.

Thus, if I exhausted every means of trying to locate these souls-on-the-wing (this being the 70s, many phone calls and phone book scratchings later), I would get to OPEN the packages, and, CSI-like, try to ascertain the whereabouts of the recipient by something in their contents.

Guess what? People send interesting items through UPS. Tear gas, for example. Firearms. Naughty things, like a case of dildos. Jewelry. It was a diverting job, for a while; too bad it didn't keep me out of the casinos.

Zack neither. We loved the glitz and glitter, the silver dollars raining down in the steel trays, the pull of the slot handles, the flick of cards at blackjack. Modern video slots, with their endless badgering combinations, their electronic payouts, their credit card readers, just aren't the same. So, even though we were working at well-paying jobs—Zack was washing the trucks and doing basic maintenance to get them ready for the drivers—neither of us put away much money.

For a while we lived at Colleen's place. Joyce and Janet even visited us there on a road trip, which was bliss for me. Zack and I moved into a place on the edge of the desert, a duplex where the owner had a bit of land, where he had an old rooster running around, a nighthawk in a cage, a goat named Jane (who we used to bring in the house, to our and Jane's astonishment), and a black cat, who was good friends with the rooster.

We'd lived there for a while when we saw a beast-in-the-jungle incident in the back yard, where our landlord and one of his friends, drunk, decided to cut the head off the rooster. They weren't going to get any savory wings off that bird, but they were crazed, and managed to cut through its neck so just some sinews held his head while he ran around.

Later, we saw the cat with the rooster's head in its mouth, running wild-eyed though the yard. They really had seemed like good buddies in the time we were there, so it was horrifying to see. I didn't think I'd ever run around with Zack's head in my mouth, but you never know.

Besides getting into people's personal packages at UPS, I also witnessed some bad behavior by the UPS drivers: at least two of them were popped for opening packages to steal expensive jewelry. One guy did it with a Rolex, which he wore to work. Now, I always kept my stolen briefcases hidden in my closet. Of course a missing Rolex sent through UPS would be tracked. I made some dumb moves as a thief, but those were glaring, and both guys lost their jobs.

Zack and I kept our jobs, but we kept playing blackjack too. We even bought a card-counting system through the mail, I think for $100. We worked on it a fair amount with each other at home, and indeed we both improved in the ability to tell when the cards were "ten-rich," or when there were higher chances of bust cards to come.

This was back in the time when Vegas had a lot of single-deck tables in many casinos, where the card-counting could be more favorable to a player. But clearly, we weren't all that good, despite us congratulating each other on our savvy. We'd sometimes win a bit, but we always came back to the trough, where the basin was usually dry.

This next circumstance probably wouldn't happen in pandemic times—though with the amount of alcohol flowing it might—but if you want to witness the vast range of creature-like human behavior in close quarters, be in downtown Vegas on New Year's Eve. I can only liken it to the photos I've seen of VE Day in Europe and the U.S., with people staggering around the streets, making out with each other and with fire hydrants, screeching to the heavens and the hells, deciding they were best friends with someone while picking their pockets.

A fine time would be had by all, but that memory would stay in Vegas, because your sodden brain could never retrieve it the next day.

Speaking of sodden brains, here's an incident that exemplifies Vegas—or indeed, a chunk of the country in the mid-70s: Zack and I were out to eat dinner in a casino restaurant, nothing overly fancy, but not that casual; a place for button-down shirts and stain-free pants. We chatted with our waiter, a guy near our ages, a couple of times before the order arrived.

He stopped by the table again and asked, in a soft voice, if we had any pot. Those indeed were the days when a certain looseness prevailed. I might not accept the offer of a drink of water from a stranger in the sweltering desert today, but then? We were all in this together.

And we did happen to have a couple of rolled joints with us. We gave those to him, he was grateful, and we knew our meal wouldn't be poisoned. But when he returned with our food, he set a small bottle, with some wet cotton inside, on the table and said, "Amyl. Take a snort."

Now I'd heard of amyl nitrite before, though in a pill form that you cracked under your nose, the quintessential "popper." But neither Zack nor I had tried it. But as I said, these were loose times. I uncapped the bottle, took a good inhale, and Zack did the same.

Well. This is not a drug you want to do when you are explaining technical investment strategies to your employees. Think of it this way: your brain before amyl is a coach sitting idle at the station. After amyl, your brain is an eight-team Pony Express ride being pursued by bandits over thrashing roads, reins lost.

The stuff has a couple of medical uses—and distinct sexual ones. One prescribed use is to relax blood vessels to increase the supply of blood and oxygen to the heart during an angina attack. That blood hammering toward your heart (and away from your head) can make your blood pressure plunge, make your head into a floating balloon, and make you warm and cozy all over. Sort of.

And it happens instantly. Whoosh! Luckily, the effects are only there for a couple of minutes, but oh my! I stared at the regular folks forking in their meals while I was riding on Santa's sleigh upside-down, my vision filled with stars and sparkles.

And then it was over. The waiter came by, smiled, and took his bottle. Zack and I mumbled a couple of mangled "wows," ate our meal, left him a tip, and left wondering why they don't put seat belts on restaurant chairs.

I didn't try my hand at pilfering in Vegas, or at least on any concerted level. Vegas is a place that has a significant percentage of security guards at every establishment, and lots of cops and plainclothes folks. But Vegas did steal most of my money from me, undoubtedly cosmic retribution for my prior work. Normal work, of course, was always unpalatable to me. So many months as the bad, bad address clerk at UPS was wearing me down, and I applied to Sonoma State, the little liberal arts college in California's Sonoma County for the fall semester of '76, and was accepted. Zack decided to stay on in Vegas for a bit.

But even though I left Vegas broke, I did leave with something: a car. And it didn't cost me a dime—until later. It was given to me and Zack right on the freeway spot where we picked up its frustrated driver. He'd left it for dead: a serviceable '65 VW bug that simply had some problem with its coil wire. I was later able to legally register it—under something like an "abandoned vehicle" statute—as mine. Later, I drove it to Sonoma State, where I began college. I used it there for several months, so that I no longer even considered how oddly it had been acquired; it was my car. You'll have to wait on tenterhooks to find out the spectacular way that car was taken from me.

There was a big (big) footnote to our stay in Vegas that happened a couple of years later, long after we were gone. My sister's husband Terry, the ever-so-straight head dude at UPS Vegas, flipped his carefully groomed wig one day, with an act that put my shoplifting career to shame: He'd received a notice that he had completed his task in Vegas and was needed back in LA. He knew my sister did not want to go back to California, and he magnified it in his mind that he was going to lose his job.

He had full access to the company safe, in which they kept a good deal of cash. He borrowed a cool $30,000 or so. He'd gone to the office on the weekend for this deed, and his entry had triggered the sprinklers and probably a burglar alarm, which, this being a case of interstate commerce, brought the FBI to my sister's house, since Terry was a prime suspect.

They interviewed Terry in their living room, with my sister there, spending about an hour. He said he knew nothing; he denied all. Several days later he flew the coop, leaving a note for Colleen on the kitchen counter saying he had to leave, and that his car was at the airport with a note in it.

That note said he had taken $2,000 because he and my sis had debts (news to my sister), and that he was trying to put the money back in the safe when the sprinklers went off, flooded the floor and evidently made the remaining money look like pea soup. He wasn't heard from again for more than five years. He spent time in the North Sea oil fields, Canada, maybe Mars.

The crazy thing was that he and my sister had been getting along—their marriage was basically solid. Not so much so after that. She divorced him in absentia some time later, long before he returned. UPS didn't really even prosecute him on his return, because there was no incontrovertible proof that he'd taken the $30,000, but also likely because they didn't want the publicity that one of their execs would saunter out of the office with a bundle. He was made to do some kind of minor community service and pay back the $2,000 that he admitted to taking. See, confession works!

That probably should have inspired me to a higher criminal ambition, but I was out of practice as a thief. And I was about to become a nice college boy again. But I did have a phase that included several last hurrahs for my happy hands.

CHAPTER THIRTEEN

Aren't You a Bit Old for That Bulge Under Your Shirt?

I arrived at Sonoma State, in the small Northern California city of Rohnert Park, with a stolen—read on—car, clothes and personal stuff. Fleeced by Vegas and a while before financial aid would kick in, I only had enough dough for a little food and gas. The gas wasn't a big deal, because I didn't have any place to go. And I literally didn't have a place to sleep. Necessity intervened.

The first night I was there, I slept in the car. This is not compatible, in the spacious confines of a VW bug, with being a bit over 6'2" and with the beginning of a bad back even then. The next six nights I slept in a sleeping bag behind some bushes and trees near the picturesque duck pond, reminiscent of Zack's and my parkland sleeping after our spectacular eviction.

After a week or so, I got a work-study job at the library, where I would work for the next four years (or really, five, since I quit school after a couple of years to go back to my working-class roots and become a house-painter. Oh wait, right—I don't have authentic working-class roots). But I did quit and paint for a while. Regardless, I had secured a lucrative—not—position in the library, though I wouldn't be paid for a month.

When my financial aid did kick in, a double-scoop of it had to go to my first month's rent and security deposit for a room out at an old, open-only-in-summer resort property in Kenwood, about a half-hour drive through the hills from the school. My housemate was an odd young man who was enthralled by the ideas of the Russian philosopher Gurdjieff. He was also the first person I'd seen who could use nunchuks as a serious weapon, demonstrating that to me with Bruce Lee rapidity on the shredded-bark trunk of a resort tree. Nonetheless, he was a pleasant guy.

Thus, I had some semblance of stability. But my pockets were picked by the move-in expenses, the income pennies from my job were a month out, and I had books and food to buy. Or did I? I did not: I had books and food to steal. I will remind you that in these heady days of criminality, bookstores—at least this college's bookstore—had yet to implement those metal detection strips that unless deactivated would trigger alarms when you passed through an RF-receiver turnstile.

Ironically, not that long later, one of my library jobs was to install those strips into what seemed to be a random selection of library books. But the bookstore? Fair game. Or unfair game for them, because all my past work of putting objects in bags and backpacks and under my arm, though underutilized for a couple of years, came easily back to the fore. Once you learn to ride a bike ...

The same goes for the cafeteria, using the old "Buy something cheap and trivial at the cashier while your backpack is stuffed with sandwiches and other bounty" trope. So, instead of asking my parents for help, I stole all of my first semester's textbooks from the bookstore, and also stole daily food out of the cafeteria. Now that I was a semi-mature adult, it didn't take me long to feel some tingle of shame and no small amount of embarrassment, but I did my deeds anyway. Not knowing anyone in front of whom to flaunt my skills, I was showing off for me, with that blend of pride and guilt.

But when I started getting regular, albeit skimpy, checks from the library, I quit my wayward ways. I was on the path of reformation. But I apparently wouldn't be driving that path, because fate wanted to toy with me a bit.

A couple of months into my first semester, a uniformed police officer came to my English class and asked for me by name. I figured that it was my hair that had probably broken some law (my 1976 hairdo was very expressive). No, it seems I was in possession of a stolen car, of all things, and that I'd have to come to the station and straighten it out.

It was easily straightened out: My VW, the car Zack and I had been given and legally registered, wasn't actually available to give. The car was owned by a woman in Vegas that had just loaned the car to our freeway doofus, and she'd discovered his poor stewardship upon her return from Japan, where she'd been touring with an entertainment group. Her particular talent was removing clothing from the profound grounds of her architecture.

Zack and I had found a manila envelope in the trunk of the VW of black and white glossies of her in/out of costume; she might put you in mind of Elly May Clampett after five vodka tonics, wearing a mail-order Lady Godiva wig. Until the cop cruised in and I got the backstory, both Zack and I were baffled about those photos.

Her name was (and might still be) Angel Blue. Under her name, the tag line on the glossies read: The Heavenly Body. As Dave Barry says, I am not making this up. And neither were the cops, who despite my protestations (and my registrations), took the car and gave it to Ms. Blue's lawyer, who had tracked me to my academic lair.

The real question I wanted answered was this: what was a stripper of Lady Blue's talents doing with a '65 Volkswagen? This was a woman that should have been driving a '59 Caddy, pretty in pink. Ah, America. My housemate, who worked in Santa Rosa, picked me up and drove us home. And he took me back and forth from school for a while, until my brother, the brother whose first motorcycle I used to unhook the speedo cable on and steal for joyrides, that brother, gave me his Yamaha 250 to use while I was carless.

That was a fine thing. It was a beautiful ride down winding rural paths from Kenwood to the school. It was also getting beautifully cold, so I soon bought a head-to-toe zip-up jumpsuit, a heavier jacket and heavy gloves. But when I got off that thing in the early mornings after my ride it took a few moments to realize that I was not a polar bear, and to persuade

my joints to bend. Colder yet was the next fall and early winter, when I was still riding the bike and I took a temporary
bottling job at Chateau St. Jean winery outside of Kenwood.

But by that point I was living across the county in Sebas-
topol. The bottling line shift was from around 6pm to
midnight, so riding home 40 minutes or so in those cool nights
was invigorating. No, it was murder. I had a tiny kerosene
stove in my tiny house and would huddle in front of it for another 40 minutes to come back to life.

There was some thievery going on in the bottling line, but
I was innocent. Chateau St. Jean had a small bottling line that
required a lot of manual help. I was the guy who took boxes of
empty bottles at the start of the line, dumped them upright in a
cluster, and then they were nudged into single-file by me and
the conveyor mechanism. They'd go under the filling nozzles,
get filled to a distance up the neck, and move on to the rag-
bearing bottle-strokers (whose whole job was to make sure the
bottle was dry) and then to the labeling machine, which also
had an assigned employee.

Best job: quality control, which meant that you made sure
the bottles were properly filled. Which they often weren't, because the dispensing machine hiccupped now and then, so that
a bottle would only be two-thirds full. The two (shades of my
refinery work) QA guys were supposed to run that unfilled
bottle back behind the filler so it would be properly filled.

Which they did. But only after they'd poured themselves
a splash of the wine into the paper cups they kept in their in-
spection area. This happened many times during a multi-hour

shift. You don't need to be a scientist to figure the result: these guys got positively blasted, every night. On some nights I thought I wouldn't make it home because I'd freeze to death. But those guys? How was it that they kept making it back in, after wobbling to their cars near midnight, in a shambles? Only God knows.

The bottling job only lasted a month or maybe a bit longer, and that was fine with me. I did manage, while doing the end-of-work cleanup, to break a five-gallon bottle of wine that was resting on the ground with some other big bottles. Moving it cracked it against another at its base, resulting in a lot of good wine chasing fame across the floor. I was told later that that particular bottle, something special, was worth about $400, which was probably what I made in the entire time I worked there. Too bad the QA guys weren't there: they would have licked it off the floor.

One of those golden ironies occurred the second Christmastime at school, when I hitchhiked home to Long Beach. My five-finger discounting was in deep remission by then, but I decided to write a short story based on my going to jail for stealing the Chivas Regal. It was the longest story I'd written to that point, though I can't give you the word count, since I wrote it in longhand. This was well before I started using a computer, and though I knew how to type and could have written it in the library, I chose to write it at home. (Incidentally, not long after that I bought a GIANT Remington typewriter, surely from Mark Twain's era, that weighed approximately 300 pounds. It was not electric.)

I brought that short story with me on my trip down south, tucked into a giant WWII suitcase that my dad had owned and had given me to go to college. So, I had a high percentage of my clothes and personal belongings (including my only dress shoes) and that story in the suitcase that ended up being pirated away by a scoundrel at the famed Andersen's Pea Soup in Buellton, about 30 miles north of Santa Barbara.

I'd been hitching north of Buellton off Highway 101 for a while and had been chatting with another hitchhiker, a guy a bit older than me, who was on the road from somewhere in the Midwest. He had a giant duffle bag that might have been Army-issue, which he mentioned had all of his belongings in the world. We were both happy when a guy in a cherry Malibu convertible picked us both up.

I didn't like the guy right off because he immediately went into a spiel about what a successful salesman he was, hinting that he was mighty successful with the ladies too. He also looked smarmy, somewhere in his mid-thirties with a Clark Gable-style mustache and slicked-up hair. But when he offered to buy us lunch at the famous pea soup restaurant—a joint I knew about, but had never tried—we both happily agreed.

I don't know what Andersen's is doing now with that soup, but in those days, they used to offer a free lunch if you ate something like 10 bowls of the soup. I doubt there were that many free lunches, because the soup had a soulmate in wet cement: it wasn't that it was terrible, it was just that it was *very* filling. Like eating a tractor tire.

I love soup and bread, but I could barely finish a bowl; neither could my fellow hitchhiker. But our intrepid salesperson managed, despite his small stature, to eat two-and-a-half bowls. Then he went to the restroom. And unbeknownst to us, he then went out the back door, to his car and down the road. With my suitcase and the duffle bag.

We waited at the table for quite a while; the waitress came over twice. I finally went back to the empty bathroom, back to the dining room, and then out to the parking lot. No convertible. So, besides stealing all of our belongings, he'd left us with the check. The manager of the place was sympathetic, and didn't charge us. She also called the cops, who, even though there aren't many side roads between Buellton and Santa Barbara that went anywhere, couldn't manage to find that weasel on Highway 101.

There's an old Ram Dass saying, "If a pickpocket meets a saint, he sees only his pockets." Well, I wasn't a saint, but that thief saw a big suitcase and went with it. The true hurt was that the other hitchhiker was left with nothing except a little cash. He was actually discussing getting a job at the restaurant with the manager when I wished him well and left. I was just a couple hours from my house, and could hitchhike home easily and tell my sympathetic parents my tale of woe. My mom was lucky in some ways because most of my suitcased clothes were dirty and she would have insisted on washing and folding them for me, big boy though I was.

On that clothes issue: our mustachioed thief was about five-seven, so none of my clothes or my shoes would have fit him. Mr. Duffle Bag was several inches taller than Convertible Man too. I guess I knew how those folks in Signal Hill felt going to their cars in the morning and opening their hoods and seeing that the reason the damn things wouldn't start was that their carburetors were missing. So maybe karma did play a part, but my take has always been that the randomness of the universe will poop on anybody now and then. Though I might have deserved it more than most.

One quick aside about my hitchhiking back: On my last ride, coming in to Long Beach, I was picked up by a couple of big, hairy guys in a pickup. Because I was a tall hairy guy, even in the large cab of this big pickup, with me in the middle, three of us abreast was tight. The first thing I noticed during the ride was that the passenger floor of the pickup had a bunch of empty beer cans on it, which the passenger-side hairy guy clunked around in.

The second thing I noticed was that both guys had open beers. The third thing I noticed, not long after being picked up, was that the driver—and I tried not to look that closely—was doing something in his crotch with his beer can with one of his hands. That something was that he was peeing in the open can, which took a lot of maneuvering, particularly while driving.

When he finished, he left-handedly winged that can of beer pee past my chest, past the passenger-side guy and out the right-side open window. That's when I noticed that the big tattoo he had on the inside of his wrist that I'd been trying to read said "FUCK" in all capital letters. (I was interested in typography then, and noted that he'd chosen Helvetica, which I thought was weak.)

At the time, and even though I myself looked like a back-alley dweller, I thought this guy was quite an outlier.

That short story I wrote? Never saw it again. But segue about 25 years into the future. Man (that being me) in a fiction-writing class stares numbly at blank page. The assignment was something like, "Take an abstract emotional concept, such as hate, love, pain, guilt, whatever, and construct a lead character who is the deepest embodiment of that abstraction, but bring that character to life."

That gave me all the motivational push of cooked cabbage, but after stewing a bit, a tangential theme bubbled up: present a character who is temperamentally (and declaredly) *devoid* of the ability to experience a certain emotion. That character: me. Or a certain exaggerated flavor of me, that being the fellow who in his heady shoplifting days would blithely toss off statements like, "I'm not stealing. I'm liberating these goods. All of these stores are just capitalist dogs preying on people."

A more mush-mouthed version of Soggy-Headed Robin Hood probably couldn't be found, but the thought of those silly spoutings put me in mind of a character who thought that if he didn't consciously admit of his feelings—in this case, guilt—those feelings didn't exist.

I set to work. I made my protagonist, Douglas, an aloof, hyper-intellectualized, Nietzsche-spewing Catholic high school student, who was an expert shoplifter. He sets up a series of shoplifting "experiments" (escalating in their bravado), which he calmly executes, and then he returns to his home with the goods, where he calculates the value of his thieving and the dearth of his emotional response.

The chink in his armor came in the form of a naïve (and fetching) young classmate who is intrigued by Douglas's odd manner, and who begins a casual flirtation. Douglas decides to incorporate her into his experiment, theorizing that he needed a vulnerable human element to show his true transcendence over guilt. The story had a lot of symbols—forgive me—and a motif critical to its sad end.

When I'd finished the story, I thought it was good enough for presentation in class, though I worried that I'd created a lead character with such exaggerated skills and morbid self-fascination (and, oh dear, based on *me*) that he would be a kind of straw man, dead on the page. However, it went over fairly well with my classmates, with some caveats.

I left the story alone for more than a year, until I read about a short story contest at the National Steinbeck Center in Salinas, only a half-hour from my home. I debated whether it was worth paying the application fee to send the story in, because I was flat certain it didn't have a chance of winning, particularly because the judge was John Steinbeck's son,

Thomas, also a writer. Though I recognized that they weren't asking that the stories be written in the tang of Steinbeck, those dark voices in my writer's head told me that my themes were too far off base to win, place or show.

My shock was tangible when I got the call that I'd won the first-place prize: $1,000 and a luncheon at the Steinbeck Center, with an award presentation from Thomas Steinbeck. I was still in a haze a week later when I went on stage to accept a beautifully engraved glass plaque, a certificate, the check and a warm handshake from Leon Panetta, Bill Clinton's former Chief of Staff and a local resident who had been a last-minute substitute for the ailing Thomas Steinbeck. That was more than 20 years ago, but I still look at that plaque with a flush of pride and happiness.

The prize was a confirmation that I did have the stuff to craft a story, and also an admonition to press forward with my writing, despite all of the night sweats that writers have over the merit of their work. (Not that, of course, pressing forward means those night sweats will go away—just that they can be showered off before you hit the keyboard again.)

Oh, I almost forgot: Some years after graduating from Sonoma State, I was working in a used record store in Santa Cruz. I was desperate to take out a woman who worked in the cookie store next to the record shop to a semi-fancy restaurant. But as usual, I was low on dough. So for several days running, it may have even been a week or two, I didn't actually ring up select customers who bought records, just opened and closed the till (which these days will often be electronically recorded), and I pocketed the cash.

It was probably $50 total or so, and I did feel pretty guilty about that. But the cookie store clerk had been so generous with giving me bags—bags!—of broken but delicious cookies that I took home to my grateful housemates, Zack and Matt and Kelly. You see, that sweet tooth from my childhood still consumed me.

One small irony at the record store: there were (and still are) a lot of bedraggled types hanging out on the streets of Santa Cruz. I know, I have been one myself. One time I was working with my boss in the store and some guy with no shop-lifting style grabbed some records and bolted. My boss told me to chase him and for about half a block I did. And then I stopped. And then I laughed to myself, thinking of chasing me down that same block and what I would do if I caught myself. When I came back in, I told my boss that he'd slipped away around a corner.

After a while, I tired of the cramped nature of the store and the work, but not before I took a blow there, which again may have been more karmic payback: I'd been given a lovely 1911 gold Elgin pocket watch from my father a long while back, who'd been given it from his father, who're received it from *his* parents when he graduated from high school. It was my most cherished worldly object, so even though it didn't pair all that well with my Levis, I did loop its beautiful gold chain though my belt loop and into the little watch pocket of my 501s.

Until that chain broke at work and I left the watch behind the shallow counter, partially under a shelf, but in plain sight. Whoever stole the watch probably only saw it for a moment, saw me putting albums away, and snatched it and walked out. I have many good memories of my father, so I felt crappy I'd let that watch get away, and to a thief yet. Were I able to go back in time to that record store, it wouldn't be any rare vinyl I'd be after: I'd go back to the very day my watch broke, and put it right in my pocket. Maybe I'd even return the money I'd stolen. Maybe.

Sometime after I'd written this chapter, I realized that my allegedly "final" college thefts, the capper to my carbonated magnum of crime, weren't the culmination after all. Underscoring the way memory works, or doesn't, I got a late-arriving synaptic letter reminding me that after I graduated from Sonoma State, I sought a new start in a suburb outside Seattle, staying under the good graces of my brother and sister-in-law.

They were both gainfully employed homeowners; I was, well, that guy I'd been for most of my life. I left Sonoma State with the same empty wallet I'd left Vegas years earlier. But I was looking for work in Seattle, so I could contribute something. One problem: I had some almost-acceptable dress clothes, but all of my shoes were either basketball shoes or flip-flops. Interview material? That would be a no.

One does fall back on their old skills when pressed, and I was pressed for dough, and too embarrassed to borrow. Necessity, the motherfucker of bad intentions.

So, I found myself at the Seattle Nordstrom Rack, the discount face of the somewhat upscale Nordstrom brand. And I found myself in the shoe department, empty of salespeople when I was there. And I found myself putting on a pair of nice leather loafers, which—miracle!—they actually had on the shelves in my size. And I found myself putting those on, and leaving my scuffed high-top basketball shoes discreetly tucked away in the corner of the lowest shelves.

And then I found myself outside the store. For a long while, my hands were clean, and I thought that would be the last thing I stole. Ironic that Barefoot Boy would steal shoes. However, I mentioned that memory thing before, so stay tuned.

By the way, I did get the job, as an entry-level copywriter for an outdoor equipment manufacturer and retailer. My first real writing job, for which they paid me money, of all things. Oh, and those miniature-but-high-powered binoculars that I brought home from there for my brother? Not stolen, nuh-uh. But they were given to me by the in-house photographer (who had a minor fancy for me) who'd used them for a product demo and who told me they couldn't be sold then anyway. She did offer—who was I to turn her down? So shoot me.

There is a short story by Edgar Allan Poe titled "The Imp of the Perverse." Poe often wrote thrillingly about scalawags, ne'er-do-wells and the shadow side of human nature. The story notes people's leanings toward irrational and often anti-social acts—the impulse toward self-sabotage. We of course have an instinct toward self-preservation (and my goodness, we will sometimes crawl all over other beings to assure it), but conversely, within many of us there are urges to do the wrong thing.

In the story, the first-person narrator has committed a perfect murder, but after years of glowing in that satisfaction, he has a perverse urge to confess. So here the self-sabotage is not the murder, but the revealing of it. Poe's thesis shows up in some of his other stories, so much so that I used his work as a model for the smug character in the Steinbeck story winner I mentioned a bit back. Here are a couple of my story's first paragraphs:

"Poe's overall theme is damnation," he said in a flat tone. "The Raven has just a taste of what Poe's all about. Why does the man poke out the cat's eye in The Black Cat? Why does the man kill the old man in The Tell-Tale Heart? Because they are perverse and they are damned. And by extension, we are all damned."

The boy slowly ran his fingers through his thick black hair and looked away, his odd, milky-gray eyes scanning the empty courtyard.

He rubbed his dark whiskers, not seen on his classmates' soft faces, and looked back to the classroom. "It's so obvious," he said.

Well, obvious to him. Of course, he was courting the perverse all along, and gets his comeuppance in the end. My comeuppance has been more gradual. Though I'm far from the haloed altar boy in my Catholic grammar school, I still feel the pangs of many of those deeds from so many years ago. Mostly from the acts that crossed the dubious line I'd established of fucking with the establishment. I wasn't stealing the establishment's carburetors, I was stealing from some person. But back then, I could rationalize both types of acts with the best of them.

One could look at this book as a confession, an act that was regularly scheduled in my Catholic upbringing, though this book lacks the two-room confessional closet, the priest behind the veiled screen, murmuring, and the alarmed boy trying to come up with a coherent litany of his crimes. Hey, I'm probably playing both priest and confessor here, now that I think about it. I'm uncertain if three Hail Marys and two Our Fathers will do their exoneration work this time though.

Though so many of those deeds at that time weary me now (ugh, hitting that guy with the giant malt on the corner), it's probably obvious I still get a frisson thinking of what I got away with, and the brazenness of many of the acts. I'll go literary on you again: the first time I read Dostoevsky's *Notes from Underground*, I was thrilled by the descriptions of the beleaguered narrator, who describes his toothache in the most voluptuous—but self-indulgent—terms. He has a bitter tooth-ache, but it's unlike any toothache of a regular man.

My thieving could be likened to that: great bravado and show, but really, just a kid indulging in petty theft. As I've by this point wearily stated, I always justified it as not stealing from people, but from faceless entities, the corporate man. That made it bigger than it was. It probably sounded as lame at the time as it does now, but now I hear the lameness more clearly.

I won't marshal this as an excuse, but part of my moral vagrancy was in trying to set myself apart: apart from the bland suburbs of my upbringing, apart from being a good boy. I wanted to be edgy in some way, though rebelling against the suburbs sounds like the edginess of not mowing the lawn every two weeks.

And feeling empty at times, as I suspect most people do, doesn't necessitate the kind of thrill-seeking I sought. I could have designed ant farms, chess pieces shaped like biblical figures, or more true to my biology, a faster-melting chocolate.

And in this time of Black Lives Matter moments, I have to account for my privilege: what if I were Black? Would I have even been able to roam freely in the stores I frequented without greater scrutiny? Would I have had much rougher treatment at the hands of the plainclothes and uniformed cops I dealt with, or the jail personnel? Things might have gone poorly for me, if not for being the scruffy but oh-so-white kid.

For me, crime paid, but not that much. I didn't have a mentor to counsel me in white-collar crime, so I went blue.

I'm sure I'm qualified to write amusing (and much more lucrative) bitcoin ransomware messages now, but I don't have the stomach for it.

For long, long years now, I don't think I've swiped anything bigger than a company pen from work. And since I've basically worked for myself the past 25 years, everything was swiped in plain sight. Regardless, I couldn't do now what I did back then anyway. Changes in theft-detection technology will keep old-school thieves like me at bay: Walmart has tested using AI-powered cameras in 1,000 stores to prevent theft, though many businesses have backed off from facial-recognition technology because of poor accuracy, particular with people of color. I understand there are other AI-based systems to quickly detect odd or criminal behavior in stores. Technology, it's a bitch.

Despite the fact that my first experience running a business was a successful one, I realized long after that my business principles were a touch compromised. Though as is clear here, my double-dealing was many, many years ago, I still wonder about the strange, amoral reaction I had to my endeavors. As suggested above, maybe I did it because I had a comfortable middle-class existence and wanted some cheap thrills, maybe I enjoyed the sense of power it gave me, maybe I wanted to be on the margins of what I thought was straight society, maybe I liked the odd admiration I received from some peers—maybe a combination of all those things.

I do think about my father and mother, who were by the book on paying the bills, mowing the lawn, waving to the neighbors. They worked their way out of the Depression and WWII. Both of them are gone now, my mother recently, to my great sorrow. She influenced me more than anyone in the world to become a writer. I always wanted my parents to be proud of me, and in many ways they were, and said so. But this full confession wouldn't warm their hearts, so perhaps it's better that they are gone now.

My mother never found out about my shoplifting until just a few years ago, and of that only a smidgen of my crimes, and she just said "Really?" and rolled her eyes and even laughed a bit. She never heard about all the LSD and other bodily euphorias, so let's just keep our lips zipped about that, since I don't know what kind of surveillance systems they have in heaven.

My sister Colleen and I wrote a formal obituary for my mom after she left this earthly plane, and no need to put that here, but because her presence meant so much to me in life, I want to include a blog post I wrote a bit after her death:

> From my early boyhood, I always wanted to be a pro baseball player. When my limitations as a ballplayer became more evident, I thought that being a writer would be just as good (and you didn't have to try and hit a curveball). I don't have to search around for why I wanted to be a

writer—the answer is as easy as the one for why I'm around: my mother.

Since I was a toddling thing, I saw my mother reading. I saw her reading magazines and newspapers; I saw her reading books. And she wasn't reading dime-store westerns (though that would have been fine too), but big novels, books that thumped when she set them down on the living room tables. I saw her reading books, enjoying books, getting more books.

My deep thoughts at the time: "Mom likes books. Books are good."

Reading, Writing (and No Rithmetic)

So, I started reading too. She was right: books are good. The more I read, the more I wanted to write, so I started writing too. Writing is good. (Except when it gives me, as Mark Twain would say, the fantods.)

My mom continued to love reading until about 10 years ago, when her macular degeneration made words on the page a blurry mess. For a while, because she still hankered for that mess, she read with a giant magnifying glass, slowly but steadily, until that became too hard as well. I've written a number of books, and she had them all, even those published after she'd stopped reading. She loved books, after all.

She died at her assisted-living home in mid-June, 2020, after a stroke in late April. She was a remarkably kind and good person, funny and chatty, and fond of social gatherings and people in general. Even though she was 97, and lived a long and good life, it's still a shock to have her gone. Whatever part of her I have is the best of me.

Thanks mom, for opening up the world of words, and all of their enchantments, to me. I hold you in my heart forever.

Only sometime after my mom's funeral, in the Catholic church of my boyhood, did it come to me how comfortable I was at the funeral Mass, the congregation in the pews, the movements of the priest, the muffled noises, the altar I'd looked at a thousand times.

Though I am far from a practicing Catholic, leagues far, all of it seemed welcoming and right to me, including discussing with the monsignor beforehand how the memorial service and eulogy would go. I didn't feel like asking him to hear a rush confession for me for all of my sins, but I took good comfort in the church and all its trappings, if not all its doctrines.

One more story before we go: sometime before Zack went to Canada for the first time, perhaps he 14 and me 15, we were riding our bikes around looking for trouble. The Long Beach Yacht Club was not that far from our house, in a cluster of small stores and boats. Not a particularly fancy place, it had a moderately large dining and meeting hall, as well as side rooms and a small kitchen.

We walked in and were intrigued to see that long dining tables were set up with shiny cutlery and nice tableware. Wine glasses, water glasses, white tablecloths. And a long table with buffet-style foods: salads cold and hot, breads, side dishes. At the center, a very large, whole cooked salmon, cut in half, one serving plate having one of the halves with the head and tail still on. And at one end, one of those giant, silver-and-black industrial coffee pots.

And no one around.

Now, it was clear that people were going to arrive, perhaps in moments. This food was ready to serve, every table was ready. Where were the servers? In the kitchen? Out front ready to greet the guests? Who knows. We couldn't hear anything. So, in this dignified setting, with no malice aforethought, we did some work.

One of us (and I do believe it was me) grabbed that large salmon by the tail, lifted the lid of that giant coffee percolator, and dropped it in. I think we replaced it with something incongruous from one of the tables or walls (maybe a sepia print of the yacht club's founder?) and we scurried out. Still no one in sight, not a peep, and us back on our bikes and heading home.

One ironic addendum to the story of my oft-partner-in-crime, Zack: he is now a national security advisor—and I have no doubt an astute one—for our government. Go figure.

I guess I can't resist, but really, just *one* more story: I wrote above about ending all of my five-finger fingerings sometime in my college years, but in considering it, there was a much more recent violation. Six or seven years ago, the little hand-towel rack in my bathroom lost the plastic plug on the side of the bar that kept it in place.

I looked online, nothing, and went to two of the big local hardware stores to get it replaced, but no dice. Then I saw a display towel rack, with the same kind of plugs, and I popped one off and put it in my pocket. I likely spend about $50 in the store for other goods, but my, was I aware of that bitty piece of plastic in my pocket. I was no longer the guy who could nonchalantly dribble a basketball out of a store with a smile.

That plug sits on my towel rack to this day, reminding me of what a world-shaking criminal I was. My guess is that that humiliation is the coup de grâce of my offender's enterprise, and I likely will do no time for the blot on my record.

I suppose you're probably tired of me trying to figure out my deeper motivation (other than being a pain) for this and other acts. The Imp of the Perverse stirred often in me in those days, for better or worse, but I suspect mostly for worse.

A while back I read a New York Times piece about a defense attorney named Bryan Stevenson, who created the National Memorial for Peace and Justice in Montgomery, Alabama, and who said in his book, Just Mercy: A Story of Justice and Redemption:

"Each of us is more than the worst thing we've ever done."

I do forgive those stupid kids we were, and the stupid kid I was. Some of the moral crimes I'll remember forever.

I guess that sounds easy, because I was rarely the offended party. What I mean is that I forgive that strange and near-inexplicable amoral leaning I had in those times. I feel guilt, and wish I could apologize for the wrongs of my ways, but I also feel sympathy for that kid trying to be a big shot, and for the oblique way he tried to both cultivate and demonstrate his bravado. He was an idiot, but he also meant well most of the time, and wished well for his fellows in the world. I won't ask *you* to forgive him, but if you see him in your stores, give him a nod (but keep an eye on him if he goes behind any tall shelves).

Anyway, no more shoplifting for me. Starting from a ways back, I've paid for my whiskey (and all those other life incidentals). Perhaps if I saw some weasel kid in a store lifting goods now, I might call the proprietors. Or I might stop him and show him a more polished technique. I hate to see a waste of talent.

However, I still would like to learn counterfeiting. So many crimes, so little time ....

Can You Take a Moment for a Review?

If you enjoyed the book, I'd be grateful if you'd review it on Amazon or Goodreads, or at your favorite online bookseller. Reviews can make a significant difference in the book's success.

On Amazon, search for *Sticky Fingers* under the Books menu; scroll down to the Customer Reviews section and there will be a "Write a customer review" button near the existing reviews. On Goodreads, after search, you can assign a star rating under the thumbnail cover of the book, and that should pop up a button giving you a chance to write a text review as well.

Or search at the online bookseller where you bought it and review it there. A review will mean a lot to me.

(Of course, reviews only need to be a few sentences or so, but please elaborate if you're of a mind to. Even if you thought the work was birdcage lining—I'm tough, I can take it.)

Stay out of your dad's wallet, and happy reading to come!

Acknowledgements

My blessings (if the blessings of a fallen Catholic are worth anything) to all of my old pals who were part of this checkered enterprise, and who let me, for the most part, recount *my* memory versions of those many escapades.

And of course, to my mother and father, who I could try to blame for all this, but no court would accept the argument. And don't forget that my siblings didn't sell me at the swap meet when they should have, so they bear some burden too.

To my editors, Jodi Fodor and Beth Balmanno, thank you, and at least I spelled your names right, right? To my cover designer, Linda Secondari and her team at Studiolo Secondari, you got me covered. (Sorry, couldn't resist. You guys did a great job.)

And to Yogi, Joyce, and Ron, rest forever in peace.

About the Author

Tom Bentley lives in the hinterlands of Watsonville, California, surrounded by strawberry fields and the occasional Airstream. He has run The Write Word, a writing and editing business, out of his home for many years, giving him ample time to vacuum.

His business projects have varied from writing website content, the full spectrum of marketing material, user documentation for software manuals, radio ads, character dialog in video games to editing coffee-table photography books.

He's published hundreds of freelance pieces—ranging from first-person essays to travel pieces to more journalistic subjects—in newspapers, magazines, and online. (Venues include Writer's Digest, Vox, Popular Mechanics, the Los Angeles Times, Writer's Market, Forbes, Wired, the San Francisco Chronicle, The American Scholar, and many others; he's also won a number of nonfiction writing awards.)

He's published short fiction in a number of small journals, and was the 1999 winner of the National Steinbeck Center's short story contest. His coming-of-age novel, *All Roads Are Circles,* was published in 2011. His short-story collection, *Flowering and Other Stories,* was published by AuthorMike Ink in early 2012. His corral-your-writing-ideas-and-get-them-to-the-page book, *Think Like a Writer: How to Write the Stories You See* was published in 2015.

His novel *Aftershock,* centered around the repercussions of the 1989 San Francisco earthquake, was published in 2018. His novel (co-written with Rick Wilson) *Swirled All the Way to the Shrub,* set in Prohibition-era Boston, was also published in 2018.

Sign up for his writing-related newsletter at http://eepurl.com/KIZuT and see his lurid website confessions at www.tombentley.com.